# La Bouche Creole II

# La Bouche Creole II

Leon E. Soniat, Jr.
June Soniat

PELICAN PUBLISHING COMPANY
GRETNA 1985

**Library of Congress Cataloging in Publication Data**

Soniat, Leon E.
  La bouche Creole II.

  Sequel to: La bouche Creole.
  Includes index.
  1. Cookery, Creole.  2. Cookery, American—Louisiana.
3. Louisiana—Social life and customs.  I. Soniat, June.
II. Title.  III. Title: La bouche Creole 2.  IV. Title:
La bouche Creole two.
TX715.S67835 1985      641.59763      85-3371
ISBN 0-88289-364-5 (pbk.)

Illustrations by Marlene Bettale

Manufactured in the United States of America
Published by Pelican Publishing Company, Inc.
1101 Monroe Street, Gretna, Louisiana 70053

# Contents

*To Leon, my dear husband, who was a man of many passions, talents, and gifts. His love for New Orleans, for Creole life, and most of all for Creole cuisine was an inspiration to me and to our entire family.*

# Preface

Those who knew him often proclaimed that Leon was a true "Renaissance man." His interests were wide-ranging and multidimensional. When he was seven years old, his family moved to an undeveloped area on the edge of New Orleans called Gentilly. Leon roamed its wild and wide-open spaces, fished in the swampy ponds, and in season hunted for rabbit, duck, and quail. His father insisted that "whatever you shoot, you will eat!" So Leon learned to clean and prepare his prizes, and in most cases he helped his mother to cook them. He boasted that he had a palate for anything that "swims, flies, or runs," and frequently tried to encourage his family and friends to give up their hang-ups about food and to broaden their horizons. In this spirit he introduced them, at one time or another, to rattlesnake meat, bear meat, smoked octopus, and fried grasshopper. He illustrated the folly of dietary prejudice with a story about a man, who, when told that the meal he was to be served consisted of beef tongue, replied that he would never eat anything so disgusting as that which came out of a cow's mouth. When asked what he did want to eat, he replied, "How about a couple of eggs?"

Leon's professional life led him to careers in radio and television broadcasting, life insurance sales, and public office. His pursuit of a career in cooking began, ironically, while he was recuperating from heart surgery. In an effort to take life at a slower pace he entered a chicken-cooking contest. He was a winner in the south-central division (his winning recipe, Chicken Carnival, is in the poultry section). The attention he received led to cooking demonstrations, a weekly column in the local newspaper, a weekly radio talk show on the subject of Creole cooking, Creole cooking classes at the University of New Orleans, and his first book, La Bouche Creole.

During thirty-four years of marriage I shared the joys and difficulties of Leon's many careers. Together we cooked for our large family, and these meals became celebrations—in a large family there is always something to celebrate! And what better way to enjoy life than with boiled crawfish, Creole jambalaya, red beans and rice, or any of a host of other family favorites?

As Leon's involvement in the whole arena of Creole cooking expanded, so did the community's interest in him. Leon was an authentic fifth-generation Creole. His television experience gave him a great platform for greeting the public, and with the publication of La Bouche Creole and his weekly newspaper columns, radio show, and cooking classes, his calendar was very full. Leon often invited me to help with food demonstrations. At autograph parties for La Bouche Creole we would cook such dishes as trout amandine, omelets, or calas. We also did some catering until we began to film his television series in our own kitchen. We did forty-three television shows, which were shown September through December of 1981.

I don't suppose anything could have tickled Leon more than having La Bouche Creole published. The books arrived in December 1980, and Leon autographed books everywhere he went. He looked forward to every opportunity to talk about Creole cuisine or to prepare Creole food, whether it was a simple dish or a five-course meal. He always enjoyed reminiscing about Memere (his grandmother) and Mamete (his mother). He firmly believed that Creole cooking, with its versatility and adaptability, was one of the great cuisines of the world.

It was with great joy and anticipation that in May 1981 we attended the American Booksellers Association convention in Atlanta, Georgia, to promote Leon's book. We continued on to North Carolina and Virginia for a lovely vacation. About one week after we returned home in June, Leon became very ill. Leon knew that Pelican Publishing Company wanted to publish a sequel to *La Bouche Creole* (roughly translated as "the Creole taste"). Contracts were signed and Leon was excited and happy at the thought of another book. He began to gather some material, but his death in August came too soon.

I knew how much Leon wanted *La Bouche Creole II* to become a reality, so I began to assemble his articles written for other publications, columns written since *La Bouche Creole* was published, recipes from his cooking demonstrations and his television programs, and some family favorites that had not been included in the first cookbook.

It is so exciting to be involved in the Creole scene—because it is such an ever-changing, alive, vibrant entity. It changes, yet some aspects of it will always remain the same. Creole cooking is to food what jazz is to music in that it accentuates improvisation on a basic theme; the technique may remain the same but the final form is not rigid. For example, we have a Creole specialty called jambalaya (which is a spin-off from the Spanish *paella*), and the only thing it must have is rice. It is said that the word jambalaya comes from *jambon* (French for ham) and *aya* (Spanish for rice). We make jambalaya with anything we have on hand—it is a good clean-out-the-refrigerator dish. If you have a little leftover ham or chicken or sausage, use it. Add shrimp, spices, stock, and rice, and that's basically it. If I lived in New England I could make it with clams and lobster or in San Francisco with stone crabs or in Alaska with reindeer sausage—it is an adaptable dish. And so the variations on a theme continue. If new things become available, Creole cooking will embrace them.

I invite readers to share any comments or questions they may have about *La Bouche Creole II*. My wish (as it was also Leon's wish) is to share our recipes and stories with you.* I present them here with a grateful heart for the deep love and affection that you have shown for Leon.


*My stories will be designated by a coffee-grinder symbol  ; Leon's will remain unmarked.

# Acknowledgments

This book would never have become a reality were it not for my wonderful family, especially my three children, Christopher, Yvette, and David, and my good friends. For their love and encouragement and help, I am most grateful.

First, I had to locate and assemble all the material and the recipes I wanted to include in the second volume of *La Bouche Creole.* I gathered recipes from our files and recipes that were favorites in Leon's family, my family, and our extended family.

My daughter Yvette and my son Chris, along with my sister Shirley Morrow and my friend Merle Guerin, helped me to "get it all together" and to arrange much of the material. I do appreciate their assistance.

For the time-consuming tasks of revising and editing, a special thanks goes to my good friend Betty Upshaw, who was such a tremendous help.

For all the typing and retyping, my thanks go to Yvette, my sister Gloria Osoinach, and my dear friend Connie Elliott. They handled most of the load, but Shirley and my daughter-in-law Nancy helped too. They are all excellent typists, and I am greatly indebted to them.

For the myriad of odd jobs, I thank my son David.

Thanks to Leon's sister Blanche Soniat Tillette, who is in her own right a superb Creole cook, and to Henri Gandolfo, longtime friend of the Soniat family. Henri is a grand resource person, and it was always fun for us to reminisce about Leon and Memere, the Soniat family, and Creole history, lifestyle, ambience, and food.

Thanks to Kate Bandos, Frumie Selchen, Karen Trahan, and Dr. Milburn Calhoun of Pelican Publishing Company for the wonderful success of *La Bouche Creole* and for undertaking *La Bouche Creole II*, and to artist Marlene Bettale for the artwork in both books.

To Ed and Debbie, many thanks for being so understanding and sharing their spouses' time with me.

Finally, a big bouquet of thanks to my children Eleanor, Leonard, and Oliver; my grandchildren; and to my friends, David Atteberry, Adele Drapekin, Cathy Soniat, Warren Fredricks, Anita Dunn, Ella Redmon, Mary Lou Christensen, Joyce Bleuler, Bee Hill, Ethel Melvin, and many others. May you all enjoy life and cooking as much as the Creole Chef always did.

# La Bouche Creole II

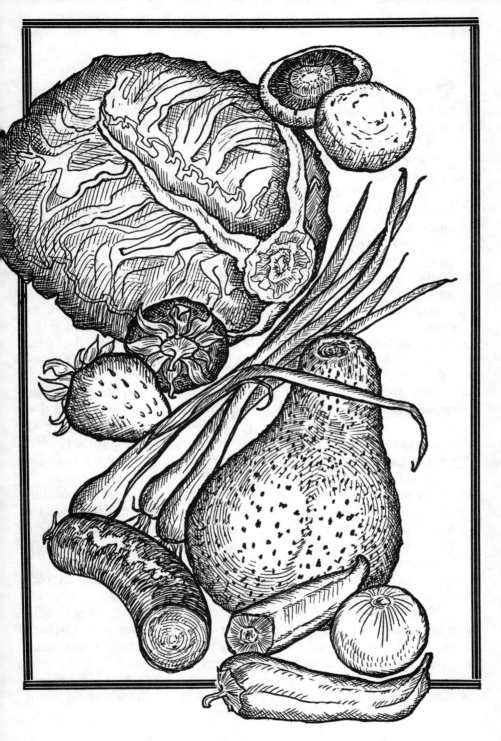

soups & gumbo

The word *Creole* means a descendant of the French or Spanish born in the colonies rather than in the mother country. The word began as a noun, but it is now used more often as an adjective, such as in Creole cooking, Creole mustard, Creole cream cheese, Creole tomatoes, shrimp Creole, and so forth. To a New Orleanian, Creole means "good."

The first thing that comes to mind when thinking about Creole food is gumbo. Gumbo is the essence of Creole cooking. With a bit of leftover ham, sausage, chicken, or duck, take a well-seasoned cast-iron pot, make a roux, add onions, bell pepper, celery, garlic, stock, and spices. Cook for a couple of hours, add filé powder (a seasoning made from sassafras leaves), serve in a bowl over hot rice, and *mon ami,* you have a hearty meal.

But what exactly is a gumbo? Well, you might describe it as somewhere between a soup and a stew. Ask any New Orleanian the question, What is the essential ingredient in a Creole gumbo? The answers will vary from sausage to okra to seafood to duck. Others will mention spices or filé.

Primarily, though, there are two groups of gumbo devotees. One group is partial to okra. Okra gives gumbo a rich, earthy flavor, and—what is equally important—a gummy substance in the okra pod thickens the stew or broth as it simmers. Years ago, okra was used only in the summer when it was readily available, but now okra is available frozen and can be purchased at any time of the year.

The second category of gumbo lovers favor the use of filé powder, another one of our important seasonings. Fresh filé powder is a beautiful green color; when packaged and purchased at the grocery store, it is slightly darker. When filé powder is used in a gumbo, it imparts a delicate flavor, somewhat similar to that of thyme, and a spoonful or so thickens stock into the kind of rich gravy that characterizes a genuine gumbo.

Many of the recipes included here are further examples of Creole adaptation. Included in this chapter are recipes for stocks, which serve as bases for gumbos and soups. And since cream soups have become popular, I have presented some of my favorites. A big bowl of any one of the vegetable soups, such as Cream of Mushroom-Artichoke Soup, Cream of Broccoli Soup, or Cream of Eggplant

Soup, would be a delicious and satisfying luncheon or dinner. Smaller portions of these appetizing soups would be good for the first course of a more formal evening meal.

As our friends and family gather together to enjoy a bowl of Chicken and Hot Sausage Filé Gumbo or a bowl of Artichoke Bisque, or Cream of Cabbage Soup along with hot and crusty French bread, it becomes a time to celebrate our being together and the bounty of the good earth. We linger with a glass of wine and share our thoughts, dreams, and news of the day's activities. And feeling too pleasantly full to move, we find ourselves reflecting on last night's good dinner or planning tomorrow's lunch or dinner.

# CHICKEN STOCK

**1 chicken, cut in pieces**　　**⅓ cup chopped celery**
**3 qts. cold water**　　　　　　**⅓ cup chopped onion**
**⅓ cup diced carrots**　　　　　**1 bay leaf**

*Place the chicken pieces in a stock pot with the cold water. Cover and bring slowly to a boil. As the stock heats, a heavy scum will rise to the surface. Skim this foamy substance for 10 to 15 minutes.*

*Add the vegetables and bay leaf; cover and simmer very gently about 3 or 4 hours.*

*Strain the stock through 2 layers of cheesecloth that have been wrung out in cold water. Cool the stock uncovered. Chill for several hours in the refrigerator. The fat will rise to the surface in a solid mass acting as a protective coating so do not remove this layer of fat until you are ready to use the stock for serving. The stock will keep in the refrigerator for four or five days. (It may also be frozen.) Yield: 2 quarts.*

# BEEF STOCK

Memere and Mamete were just about the best stock-makers who ever wielded stock pots in a Creole kitchen. The Creoles were very particular about the quality of their stocks; they set great store by the way stocks were made, and this made a lot of sense. Since a stock was the background or base on which most of the great Creole dishes were constructed, it didn't make sense, to them, to use an incorrectly made stock—it would be like an artist producing a masterpiece on a very poor grade of canvas. The stocks that they used were crystal clear, no fuzziness or cloudiness about them. They were strong and wonderfully flavored, and, when reduced, they made a marvelous jelly which made their aspics, glacés, and headcheese so delightful.

Now lest you believe it a simple task to make a good stock, let's change that opinion right now. A properly made stock is truly a work of art, requiring a number of steps which must be followed carefully. So let's follow Memere as she prepared a stock that would be used later in one of her gumbos, soups, or stews. For a BEEF STOCK, first the meat had to be washed very well. This was done to remove any "bone dust" or particles that might cloud the stock. Now the meat was put into the stock pot and covered with cold water. Remember that: *cold water*. Hot water, at the beginning, will ruin the stock, so don't dump a piece of meat and bones into boiling water and believe you're making a stock. The stock pot is put on the lowest heat possible and allowed to come to a simmer very slowly. In this way the meat and bones are allowed to release all their flavor. If the meat is added to hot water, or if the water is brought quickly to a boil, the flavor becomes locked in the meat. The old wood stoves were remarkable for producing excellent stocks because the pot could be placed on the back of the stove, where the heat was very low.

So we bring the liquid to a slow simmer—and be sure it is a slow simmer—with just an occasional bubble or two rising to the surface. You will notice a scum that will rise to the top of the water. Skim this scum very carefully, disturbing the liquid as little as possible. Oh, I forgot to mention that if you don't have a wood stove, you can use an asbestos pad or the accessory sold in our cook shops called a "flame tamer" under your pot to cut down the heat from your electric or gas stove. Now your stock continues simmering slowly; let it simmer until all the scum has been removed. This might take an hour or longer. Don't stir; in fact, don't disturb the meat at all; let it rest on the bottom of the pot. You will notice, at this point, that the liquid has remained clear, not cloudy as it would be if you kept disturbing the meat.

After the meat has quit releasing the scum, the vegetables can be added. Very gently add a whole pod of garlic (do not peel, and don't worry—a whole pod will not be too much); 2 onions, unpeeled; a scraped carrot, and a *bouquet garni* (this can be a rib or two of celery, tied with a couple of bay leaves, a sprig of thyme, and a couple of sprigs of parsley). Do not add any powdered seasonings. Let the stock cook for another 3 to 4 hours without any disturbance, then strain through a couple of thicknesses of cheesecloth and cool uncovered. You now have a stock about which you can boast.

**2½ lbs. beef shank or beef bones**
**2½ lbs. beef stew meat**
**4 qts. cold water**
**1 whole pod of garlic**
**2 onions, peeled and quartered**

**1 carrot, peeled and cut in half**
**2 ribs celery**
**2 bay leaves**
**1 sprig thyme**
**2 sprigs fresh parsley**

*Yield: 10 to 12 cups.*

# FISH STOCK

2 lbs. fish heads and bones
  (do not use an oily fish
  such as mackerel)
7 cups cold water (enough
  to cover all ingredients)
1 cup dry white wine

2 bay leaves
1 coarsely chopped onion
1 bunch green onion tops
1 chopped carrot
6 peppercorns

*Place all the ingredients in a stockpot. Heat until the liquid begins to simmer and cook, uncovered, over a brisk heat 20 to 30 minutes, skimming any scum that rises to the surface. Do not cook fish stock longer than 30 minutes or it may develop a bitter flavor. Strain. When the stock is cool, refrigerate. The stock keeps for 2 or 3 days covered in the refrigerator or you may freeze it immediately. Yield: 6 to 8 cups.*

# SEAFOOD STOCK

2 lbs. crab shells, shrimp
  shells, or crawfish shells
2 qts. cold water (or enough
  to cover all ingredients)
2 bay leaves

1 coarsely chopped onion
1 bunch green onion tops
1 chopped carrot
1 tsp. lemon juice

*Place all the ingredients in a stock pot. Bring to a boil; skim, then simmer uncovered for 20 to 30 minutes. Strain and cool. If the seafood stock will not be used within 2 days, freeze immediately. Yield: 6 to 8 cups.*

# CHICKEN AND HOT SAUSAGE FILÉ GUMBO

¼ cup vegetable oil
½ lb. chaurice sausage or any hot smoked sausage, cut in ½-inch-thick slices
½ lb. andouille sausage or any Polish sausage, cut in ¼-inch-thick slices
1 3- to 4-lb. roasting chicken, disjointed and seasoned lightly with salt and generously with black pepper
½ cup flour
4 cups chopped onion
2 cups chopped celery
2 cups chopped green pepper

1 tbsp. minced garlic
8 cups hot water
2 tbsp. Worcestershire sauce
¼ tsp. thyme
¼ tsp. ground allspice
½ tsp. basil
1 tsp. salt
3 bay leaves
¼ tsp. cayenne pepper
¼ tsp. Tabasco
1 cup finely chopped green onions
1 cup minced fresh parsley
2 or 3 tbsp. filé powder
cooked rice

*Place the oil in a heavy cast-iron Dutch oven over moderate heat and fry the sausage for several minutes, turning the sausage pieces over frequently until they are a rich golden light-brown color. Remove the sausage from the pan and set it aside. Brown the chicken in the Dutch oven and set it aside.*

*Add the flour, all at one time, to the warm oil in the Dutch oven. Stir constantly over moderately low heat for 15 to 20 minutes to make a dark brown roux. (The roux should be a pecan or nut-brown color.) Remember, the heavy pot will hold the heat. Therefore, the roux continues to cook, making it necessary for you to stop before it gets to exactly the color you wish.*

*Into the Dutch oven add the onions, celery, and green pepper, cooking over moderate heat until the onions are almost soft (about 10 minutes). To this add the garlic and stir well for about 5 minutes more.*

*Gradually add the hot water, stirring constantly, and bring to a boil over high heat. Then stir in the Worcestershire sauce, thyme,* allspice, basil, salt, bay leaves, cayenne pepper, Tabasco, chicken, and sausage. When the mixture returns to a boil, reduce the heat to a simmer and cover the pot partially. Simmer for 1 hour, then taste to adjust the seasonings.

Five minutes before removing the gumbo from the heat, stir in the green onions and parsley. Remove the pot from the heat and let it cool down for about 5 minutes, then stir in the filé powder. (Do not cook after the filé powder has been added.) You may wish to put the filé powder in a bowl for each person to serve himself. Serve over hot rice. Serves eight to ten.

# CHICKEN SOUP

Every good cook knows the therapeutic and nutritional value of chicken soup. When my two sisters and I reminisce we chuckle at our grandmother's prescription to speed our recovery from a bad cold or a flu bug or *fatigué* (just plain fatigue). Her recommendation was a warm bowl of homemade CHICKEN SOUP. She would say, "Eat, eat. You have to have strength to worry."

*To prepare the stock:*

**1 3-lb roasting chicken**
**3 qts. cold water**
**2 outer stalks celery, with leaves**

**1 carrot, cut in 1-inch pieces**
**1 medium onion, quartered**
**1 bay leaf**

Place all the ingredients in a stock pot, bring to a boil, then reduce the heat, cover, and simmer for 20 minutes. Turn off the heat, keep the pot covered, and let stand for 1 hour.

Pierce the chicken leg with an ice pick. If the juice is clear, the chicken is cooked. If the juice is red, simmer 10 to 15 minutes longer.

When the chicken is cooked, remove it from the pot and cool. Now simmer the broth until it has been reduced by one-third, then strain it and let it cool. Skim the fat off the top with a spoon. If you refrigerate the broth for several hours the fat will congeal and rise to the surface where it can be easily removed.

When the chicken is cool enough to handle, remove the skin and debone. Cut the chicken meat in large dice, cover, and set aside.

To prepare the soup:

**1 bunch watercress**
**8 cups chicken stock**
**3 cups chopped green**
**onions**
**2 cups diced cooked**
**chicken**

**2 tsp. dry sherry**
**2 tsp. soy sauce**
**3 dashes Tabasco**
**salt and pepper to taste**

Wash the watercress and discard the thick stems; break the long strips in half. Set aside.

Shortly before you wish to serve the soup, place the chicken stock in a soup pot, bring the liquid to a boil, and then add the green onions, watercress, chicken meat, sherry, and soy sauce to the broth. Season with the Tabasco, salt, and pepper. Serves six to eight.

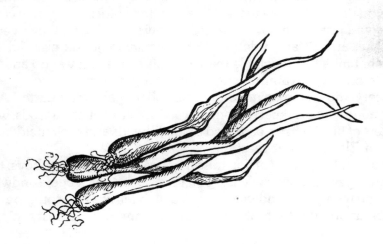

# OYSTER SOUP

The other day a friend of mine asked me an interesting question: "You write about a lot of places and customs that no longer exist today; if you could, what would you bring back? In other words, what do you miss the most?"

I thought for a minute; then I remembered how much we always enjoyed our fresh milk and bread, delivered early in the morning. That I still miss. Imagine having a milkman who delivered not pasteurized or homogenized or "Vitamin D Added" milk, but just plain old rich, creamy, raw milk—in bottles—every morning while you slept. And those crisp, crunchy loaves of French bread that you brought inside for breakfast, the ones the bakery man had left for you just a few hours out of the oven. You spread the bread with butter and dipped it into café au lait for a morning pepper-upper. And oh! that butter. I miss going to the corner grocery and buying fifteen or twenty cents' worth of smooth, yellow-golden tub butter. With his paddle, the groceryman would scrape some of the butter out of a wooden tub in the icebox and place it in a paper carton. And how about lagniappe? There was always a piece of candy or maybe a fruit that the grocer would hand you as you left his store.

Leaving food for a moment, I miss those wonderful streetcar rides that you used to be able to take. Imagine, for a fare of just seven cents you could just about cover the city of New Orleans, from the river to the lake, and sit and ride in comfort while someone else did the driving. I miss the vegetable man with his horse and wagon and his shouts of, "I got watermelons, lady . . . I got corn and beans and lettuce!" And just imagine, three dozen bananas for a quarter! And what about the blackberry women walking, straight as ramrods, with baskets of blackberries balanced on their heads and their melodious cries of Blackberrieeeeees!

I wonder how many of you miss those Martin Bros. poor boys. For a dime—yes, just two nickels—you could get a roast beef sandwich dripping with gravy and even dressed with lettuce and tomatoes. A combination about a foot long with ham and cheese cost a nickel more.

But all this is not to denigrate in any way the here and now. These are wonderful and exciting times. Except, of course, they could be better if we only had some of those things from the past. Some things do change but if you're still waxing nostalgic, one thing that is as good today as it was in yesteryear is a good old-fashioned OYSTER SOUP.

3 tbsp. butter
2 tbsp. flour
2 tender celery ribs, finely chopped
½ cup minced onion
¼ cup finely chopped green pepper
2 bay leaves
⅛ tsp. powdered thyme ¼ tsp. Tabasco

1½ cups oyster liquor (add water to liquor to make 1½ cups)
Salt and black pepper to taste
3 doz. oysters, chopped
1½ cups of half-and-half (room temperature)
1 tbsp. minced parsley

*Melt the butter in a saucepan, add the flour, and over very low heat, cook for about five minutes. Add the celery, onion, green pepper, bay leaves, thyme, and Tabasco. Cook over low heat until the vegetables are limp and transparent. Add the oyster liquor and mix well. Now add the salt and black pepper. (Remember that the oyster liquor is already salty.) Now add the oysters to the pot. Cook about 10 minutes. Remove the pot from the heat and slowly stir in the half-and-half. Return to the burner and heat to a bare simmer. When the soup is hot, sprinkle in the parsley and serve with maybe a small piece of butter in each plate. An old-time treat for your bon appetit. Serves four to six.*

# SHRIMP BISQUE

*To prepare the stock:*

**3 lbs. shrimp (with heads)**
**1 onion, coarsely chopped**
**2 cloves garlic, finely**
**chopped**
**⅛ tsp. thyme**
**½ lemon, sliced**
**2 bay leaves**
**6 cups cold water**

*Peel the shrimp. Refrigerate the meat. Place the heads and shells in a 2-quart saucepan; add the onion, garlic, thyme, lemon, and bay leaves, and cover with cold water. Bring to a boil, then lower the heat, cover, and allow to simmer gently for about 1 hour.*

*When the stock is ready, strain the broth carefully to remove all pieces of shell.*

*For a good bisque, it is important to have a good stock. Using the shells and heads of the shrimp will give a stronger flavor to your bisque.*

*To prepare the bisque:*

**4 tbsp. butter or margarine**
**4 tbsp. finely chopped green**
**onions**
**4 tbsp. finely chopped**
**celery**
**1 tbsp. finely chopped onion**
**1 lb. peeled raw shrimp,**
**finely chopped**
**4 tbsp. flour**
**2 cups warm stock**
**1 tsp. salt**
**pinch or two of nutmeg**
**¼ tsp. white pepper**
**¼ tsp. Tabasco**
**1 cup half-and-half**
**4 tbsp. finely chopped fresh**
**parsley**
**2 tbsp. sherry (optional)**

*Melt the butter in a saucepan. Sauté the green onions, celery, and onion until the onion is soft. Add the shrimp; cook over moderate heat for about 3 or 4 minutes until the shrimp turn pink. Then blend in the flour and slowly add the stock, stirring until well blended. Simmer gently for about 3 or 4 minutes. Add the salt, nutmeg, and pepper.*

Warm the half-and-half and stir into the soup. Remove from the heat. Sprinkle the parsley over the bisque, add the sherry, and serve immediately. Serves four.

## SHRIMP AND MUSHROOM SOUP WITH SHERRY

6 tbsp. butter
6 tbsp. flour
3 cups shrimp stock
2 cups half-and-half
1½ cups uncooked
   chopped shrimp
1½ cups sliced mushrooms,
   sautéed in 1 tbsp. butter
1 hard-cooked egg, finely
   chopped

1 tsp. salt
½ tsp. grated lemon peel
½ tsp. white pepper
¼ tsp. Tabasco
dash nutmeg
¼ cup dry sherry
3 hard-cooked egg yolks,
   sieved (garnish)
2 tbsp. finely chopped green
   onions (garnish)

Melt the butter in a cast-iron Dutch oven over low heat to make a blond roux. Whisk in the flour until it is thoroughly blended—this will take about 3 minutes. The flour should be a blond color—you do not want it to brown. Now, add the stock, stirring constantly until the stock and the roux are well blended. Then add the half-and-half, stirring constantly until the mixture starts to simmer. Now add the shrimp, mushrooms, egg, salt, lemon peel, white pepper, Tabasco, and nutmeg. Simmer approximately 20 to 25 minutes.

Add the sherry and simmer about 5 more minutes. Serve garnished with egg yolks and green onions. Serves six to eight.

NOTE: To obtain the shrimp stock, boil the shrimp heads and shells for 30 minutes, then strain.

# CREAM OF BROCCOLI SOUP

1 lb. fresh broccoli
3 cups chicken stock
¼ tsp. salt
¼ tsp. grated lemon rind
3 green onions, finely
  chopped
1 cup sliced fresh
  mushrooms

⅛ tsp. freshly ground black
  pepper
¼ tsp. Tabasco
2 tbsp. butter
3 tbsp. flour
2 cups half-and-half

*Soak the broccoli in cold water for 15 minutes; drain well. Remove the large leaves and the tough parts of the stalks. Cut deep gashes in the bottom of each stalk.*

*In a medium-sized saucepan bring the chicken stock to boil over high heat and add the broccoli, salt, lemon rind, green onions, mushrooms, pepper, and Tabasco. Cover the pan, lower the heat to a simmer and cook for 30 to 35 minutes until the broccoli stalks are tender when tested with a fork. Puree the mixture in a blender or food processor.*

*Melt the butter over medium heat in a large skillet and stir in the flour with a wire whisk. When smooth, add the broccoli puree and continue stirring. As soon as the mixture thickens, taste and adjust the seasoning as desired. Warm the half-and-half to 100 degrees in a separate pan, then add it to the broccoli mixture. When thoroughly mixed, turn off the heat. (If you have to reheat, do so slowly and over low heat. Watch carefully so that it does not come to a boil. Stir while it is heating to prevent from burning.) Serves six to eight.*

# CREAM OF CABBAGE SOUP

As I remember it, I learned to eat at a very early age. Now, lest you get the wrong idea, I'm not referring to the simple act of ingesting food. Oh no, as I began to learn discipline and understand the reasons for it, I became caught up in a whole new procedure that was followed, without fail, whenever the family sat down for the evening meal.

The first rule, which Memere and Mamete considered the most important to the proper enjoyment of a meal, was that never was anyone served a meal if he were perturbed or upset in any way. The meal would be delayed until everyone's disposition was as cheerful as possible.

The activity at the table would start only after the bread—for every meal there was the ubiquitous loaf of fresh French bread—had been blessed, broken, and passed around. The blessing proceeded as follows: Pepere or Papete would remove the bread from its wrapper and, with a knife, scratch a cross in the crust of the underside of the bread. The bread blessed, the meal would start.

Now came the period of passing the plates. No one served himself. The server was always Memere or Mamete, and the plates were filled with what had been cooked that day, there being no period of indecision on anyone's part as to whether he wanted some of this or that. Your plate was served and you ate what was on it. (This is probably why today there is nothing that I don't enjoy eating.) As the meal was served Pepere would pass the wine, which was present at every evening meal. Anyone less than about fifteen would be on half-rations: that is, he was given half a glass of wine, and the glass was then filled to the top with water.

You always saved a small piece of your bread to use as a "pusher." This was something that children learned very early. You didn't shove the food onto your fork with your finger; instead you used your bread pusher. Another important rule that we learned rather early was that you never requested any more food than you could comfortably eat. If you did, you sat at the table and ate every bit of what you'd asked for. You would be reminded that since your eyes were bigger than your stomach, you were going to be taught a lesson, and so you sat there until you finished. I recall one particular experience. We had boiled cabbage, and I was on my second plateful. I asked for the pepper vinegar. It was handed to me with the warning to be careful, since it was very hot. Well, I heeded not the warning, and in my youthful perversity I proceeded to shake the bottle rather vigorously. I was rewarded with a number of very strong squirts of the hot pepper sauce. I learned another valuable lesson that day, as I was made to sit and swallow every bit of that red-hot cabbage!

It was from such beginnings, I find, that even today I have certain attitudes and habits that are just about unshakable. Let me describe just one. It has been so ingrained in my nature that to waste food is a sin that, regardless of how high the food is piled, I will never leave anything but a clean plate. Really, I'm one of those few people who, when served anything on a bed of lettuce leaves, will eat all of the lettuce. Further, I also eat the parsley garnish! (It's one of the best breath fresheners in existence.) Okay, so much for the rules. Now, for the eating. Let's enjoy a delightful CREAM OF CABBAGE SOUP.

| | |
|---|---|
| **1 medium head cabbage, shredded** | **3 cups milk** |
| **3 large onions, thinly sliced** | **1 cup sour cream** |
| **1 bell pepper, minced** | **2 tbsp. flour** |
| **2 slices pimento, chopped** | **2 tbsp. butter (room temperature)** |
| **2 bay leaves** | **dash nutmeg** |
| **½ tsp. thyme** | **salt and pepper to taste** |
| **½ tsp. basil** | **4 strips bacon, fried crisp and chopped** |
| **½ tsp. celery salt** | **¼ cup grated Swiss cheese** |
| **1 qt. chicken stock** | |

*Place the cabbage, onions, bell pepper, pimento, seasonings, and stock in a soup pot. Bring to a boil and then reduce the heat. Partially cover the pot and allow the liquid to boil very gently or simmer until the cabbage is very tender and the liquid has been reduced down to about half its original volume.*

*When you are ready to serve, gradually stir the milk into the sour cream, then add the mixture to the soup. The soup pot should be over a low heat—do not let the soup come to a simmer.*

Knead the flour into the butter (this is called a beurre manié). To do this, gradually add the flour to room-temperature butter using a fork or a spoon to form a smooth paste. Add the flour-butter mixture a little at a time to the soup, stirring constantly. Continue until all the beurre manié is thoroughly mixed and blended into the soup. Then add the nutmeg, season with salt and pepper, and allow to warm for another 2 or 3 minutes. When ready to serve, add the bacon to the pot. Sprinkle a bit of the cheese in each bowl. Serves six to eight.

## CREAM OF EGGPLANT SOUP

2 small eggplants
2 tbsp. butter
2 tbsp. oil
2 onions, finely chopped
½ cup celery, finely chopped
2 large potatoes, peeled and sliced
1 tsp. curry power
¼ tsp. cayenne
¼ tsp. thyme
½ tsp. basil
2 bay leaves
1 tsp. salt
4 cups chicken stock
1 tsp. black pepper
¼ tsp. Tabasco
½ cup finely chopped green onions
1½ cups half-and-half

First peel and slice the eggplant and place in cold water in which 1 tablespoon of salt has been dissolved. Let soak for ten minutes. Rinse, drain, and finely dice.

In a heavy saucepan, add the butter and oil and, over low heat, sauté the onions, celery, potatoes, and eggplant for 15 minutes, stirring frequently. Now add the curry, cayenne, thyme, basil, bay leaves, and salt, stir well and cook 10 more minutes. Stir in the chicken stock, cover, and allow to simmer slowly for ½ hour, stirring occasionally. Remove from the heat, cool and puree in a blender or food processor. Return to the pot and over a very low heat bring to a simmer and slowly stir in the black pepper, Tabasco, green onions, and half-and-half. Bring to a simmer and serve. Serves six.

# CREAM OF TOMATO SOUP

1 28-oz. can tomatoes,
  sieved
2 onions, sliced
1 bay leaf
1 tsp. sugar
1 tsp. salt

¼ tsp. black pepper
¼ tsp. cayenne pepper
dash Tabasco
2 tbsp. butter
2 tbsp. flour
1½ cups milk

*Combine the first 8 ingredients in a 2-quart saucepan. Simmer 10 minutes, then cover and set on the top of a pot of hot water to keep warm.*

*Melt the butter in a skillet over moderate heat and add the flour. Stir constantly over moderate to low heat until well blended, about 5 minutes—you don't want it to brown. Now add the milk and whisk until well blended and thickened.*

*Slowly add the warm tomato mixture, continuing to stir. Serve immediately. Serves six.*

# OLLIE'S BEAN SOUP

Ham bone with enough
  meat on it to equal 1 cup
  of ham, finely chopped
1 lb. dry white navy beans
1 onion, coarsely chopped
2 ribs celery, coarsely
  chopped
2 cloves garlic, minced
4 qts. water
½ tsp. black pepper
¼ tsp. cayenne pepper

½ tsp. white pepper
dash Tabasco
1 bay leaf
½ tsp. dried thyme
1 bunch green onions, finely
  chopped
2 carrots, grated
1 tsp. salt
2 tbsp. minced fresh parsley
  (garnish)

*Cut the ham from the bone. Put the ham bone, the ham, beans, onion, celery, and garlic in a heavy pot with the water. Bring to a boil* over high heat, then lower the heat to a simmer. Add the black, cayenne, and white peppers, Tabasco, bay leaf, thyme, and stir well.

Simmer for 2½ hours. Add the green onions and carrots, stir well and taste before you add the salt. Adjust the pepper seasoning and continue to simmer for 30 minutes or until the soup is a bit thick.

Serve the soup in bowls and garnish each bowl with the minced parsley. Serves eight.

# CREAM OF MUSHROOM-ARTICHOKE SOUP

¼ cup butter
½ cup green onions, finely
  chopped
2 ribs celery, finely chopped
1 carrot, finely chopped
3 tbsp. flour
1 qt. chicken stock
salt and black pepper to
  taste

2 bay leaves
¼ tsp. thyme
¼ tsp. Tabasco
1 14-oz. can artichoke
  hearts, undrained
½ lb. sliced fresh
  mushrooms
2 egg yolks
1 cup heavy cream

Melt the butter in a heavy pot. Over low heat sauté the green onions, celery, and carrot for 5 minutes. Stir in the flour and cook for 3 more minutes, stirring constantly. Now add the chicken broth, salt, pepper, bay leaves, thyme, and Tabasco and slowly simmer for 15 minutes. Cut the artichoke hearts in quarters or eighths and add the artichokes, liquid, and the mushrooms and simmer for another 10 minutes.

Beat the egg yolks slightly and add them to the cream. Beat gently to combine. Remove the pot from the heat and stir a few tablespoons of the hot mixture into the egg and cream, mix well, then add this to the remaining hot mixture in the pot. Stir well. Serves four to six.

# ARTICHOKE BISQUE

1 stick butter
1 large onion, coarsely
  chopped
2 ribs celery, finely chopped
4 cloves garlic, minced
1 bunch green onions, finely
  chopped
6 tbsp. flour
4 cups warm chicken stock
2½ cups water

2 14-oz. cans artichoke
  hearts, chopped (reserve
  1½ cups liquid)
1 cup dry white wine
1 bay leaf
1 tsp. salt
1 tsp. white pepper
½ tsp. thyme
¼ tsp. Tabasco
4 oz. light cream

*Place the butter in a heavy Dutch oven over moderate heat. Add the onion and celery and, stirring constantly, cook until the onion is almost transparent and then add the garlic and green onions. Continue to cook over moderate heat until you smell the garlic. Sprinkle the flour into the pot and stir constantly over a moderate heat, until the flour and vegetables are completely integrated and the flour has cooked for 2 to 3 minutes. Add the warm stock, the liquid from the artichoke hearts, water, and white wine, stirring all of the time. Add the seasonings and stir well. Simmer, partially covered, for 45 minutes. Stir occasionally. Add the artichoke hearts and continue to cook on a low simmer for an additional 30 minutes. Remove the warm soup from the fire and add the cream. Serves six to eight.*

# COLD STRAWBERRY SOUP

This is a delightful way to begin a luncheon or a light summer evening supper. The soup can be followed with small cucumber, watercress, or asparagus sandwiches, or any sandwich of your choice. A light fruit salad would also complement this soup.

**3 pts. fresh strawberries,
  washed and hulled
1 cup sugar
¾ cup sour cream
¾ cup plain yogurt**

**1 pint half-and-half
1 cup Johannisburg
  Riesling wine or a fruity
  semi-dry white wine**

*Puree the strawberries with the sugar in a blender, reserving at least 6 berries for garnish. Strain through a sieve into a bowl. This is to take out the seeds. Set aside.*

*Whisk in the sour cream and the yogurt together until well blended. Now add the half-and-half, stir well, and then add the wine. Combine this with the strawberry mixture and mix well. Serve in chilled cups and garnish each cup with a fresh strawberry. Serves six.*

# SOUP MEAT

A friend remarked to me the other day that I had never given any real treatment to soup meat and the numerous ways the Creoles had of dealing with a nice chunk of brisket that had been cooked in a vegetable soup. Call it boiled beef, bouilli, or soup meat—three names for the same thing—its use as leftovers is another study in the ingenious ways the Creoles had for not wasting anything edible. Even today the rule of thumb for buying soup meat is to always buy more than you need for the soup in order to indulge your fancy in these many delicious leftover treats.

All in the family looked forward to the soup, but even more than that, we liked the meat. Just before serving the soup, the meat was removed, placed on a platter, and served after the soup with a sauce made of Creole mustard, horseradish, and cream or sour cream.

*To prepare the sauce:*

**1 tbsp. horseradish**　　　　　**salt and pepper to taste**
**6 tbsp. Creole mustard**
**½ cup heavy cream or sour**
**cream**

*Blend together well and serve with the soup meat.*

This was always the first use, but have you ever enjoyed a soup meat sandwich the next day? A few thin slices of the meat were placed between French bread and dressed with a little chopped onion, green onion, garlic, and a few smidgens of hot peppers for zing. The bread was buttered and the whole sandwich was warmed in the oven for a minute or two.

# SOUP MEAT PIE

This was another one of Memere's specialties.

3 tbsp. butter
1 tbsp. oil
4 tbsp. flour
1 medium onion, finely
  chopped
2 ribs celery, finely chopped
1 small bell pepper, finely
  chopped
2 cloves garlic, minced

¾ cup beef stock
3 cups cooked soup meat,
  cut in small cubes
salt and pepper, if needed
2 tbsp. minced fresh parsley
1 pie crust, unbaked (see
  index)
1 pie crust top (see index)

*In a heavy saucepan melt the butter and add the oil and the flour. Cook over moderate heat to make a dark brown roux, stirring the flour constantly so that it does not burn. This will take about 10 to 15 minutes. Now add the onion, celery, and bell pepper and cook over moderate heat until the onions are almost transparent and then add the garlic. Stirring constantly, add the beef stock and the cooked soup meat. Reduce the heat to low, add salt and pepper if needed, and cook for about 5 minutes. Remove from the heat, add the parsley and pour into the unbaked pie shell. Cover with the top crust and seal the edges by pressing with a fork dipped in water. Slash the top in several places to allow the steam to escape. Bake at 400 degrees for 25 minutes or until golden brown. Serves six.*

And of course there are more ways that I can think of to use soup meat in a delightful dish. Here's another one that comes to mind— SOUP MEAT SALAD.

# SOUP MEAT SALAD

2 cups cooked soup meat,
cut into ½-inch cubes
1 cup leftover rice
1 small onion, minced
4 green onions, minced
2 ribs celery, minced
1 tbsp. minced fresh parsley

salt and black pepper to
taste
3 tbsp. olive oil
1 tbsp. vinegar
½ cup mayonnaise
1 hard-cooked egg, sliced
2 tomatoes, quartered

*Put all the ingredients except the egg and the tomato quarters in a bowl, in the order given, mixing after each addition. Toss, garnish with the egg and tomatoes. Serve on crisp lettuce leaves for a delightful treat. Serves four.*

# SOUP MEAT HASH

3 tbsp. butter or bacon
drippings
3 cups raw Irish potatoes,
peeled and cut in small
cubes
1 medium onion, finely
chopped

2 cloves garlic, minced
½ cup soup broth or cream
3 cups cooked soup meat or
roast, cut in small cubes
salt and pepper
3 tbsp. minced fresh parsley

*Melt the butter or drippings in a heavy skillet. Add the potatoes, onion, and garlic and cook over moderate heat, stirring occasionally. When the potatoes are cooked add the broth or cream, the cooked meat, and the salt and pepper. Cook until the potatoes are brown. Add the parsley and serve. Serves six.*

*salads & dressings*

More than any other part of the menu, a salad invites the play of an artful imagination.

The salad can be adapted to whatever function the cook chooses. A salad at the beginning of a meal tempts the appetite; sometimes it is the main course, or it can an accompaniment or side dish. Often, after a heavy meal, the salad is used as a sorbet to cleanse the palate.

We find the crispness of raw vegetables refreshing. It's not surprising that salad bars have become so popular—salads are low in calories and high in nutritional value. We are fortunate to have fresh carrots, celery, beets, cauliflower, lettuce, and greens available in New Orleans all year. Through most of the summer months the most delicious-tasting tomato in the world, our Creole tomato (my prejudice is showing), is also available. Leon and I loved these tomatoes sliced and garnished with finely chopped fresh basil from our herb garden. We would ladle French dressing made from olive oil, vinegar, salt, and black pepper on top. This combination is so tasty that we even took bits of French bread and dunked the bread into our salad bowls so that not a drop of dressing would be wasted.

Some of our salads are made from a bountiful variety of local seafood including crabmeat, shrimp, and crawfish. These salads are often served in a scooped-out tomato or half of an avocado. Chicken salad is a also a perennial favorite.

We also have an abundant supply of such fresh fruits as mandarin oranges, grapefruit, Louisianna navel oranges, sweet strawberries, cantaloupe, honeydew melon, and watermelon. All of these contribute to delightful fruit salads.

New Orleanians have always loved salads and have had an ample supply of fresh vegetables and fruits year round from the French Market as well as the corner grocer. Salads form an integral part of the Creole menu.

# THE GREEN SALAD

The secret of a good crisp green salad begins, if you are not fortunate enough to have a garden, in the produce department of your grocery store. Nothing surpasses Bibb lettuce if it's available. I select a combination of greens—Bibb, Boston, Ruby, or Romaine lettuce. Romaine is a heavier green and adds taste and texture. Avoid buying any greens that are yellow or limp. I also use a few leaves of the stronger escarole or chicory as an accent. These have a slightly sharp taste, but that little touch of bitterness is not unattractive, and a small amount adds a tingle to the milder greens.

All these greens require a thorough cleansing to remove grit. Separate the leaves and gently break the larger leaves into bite-size pieces; remove the stalk tips or tough veins. Drop the leaves into a bowl of cold water and plunge them down several times. Transfer them to a second bowl of cold water and repeat the process. Then lift out the leaves a few at a time (pouring the whole batch into a colander to drain would trap the grit in them). Dry them carefully with toweling or in a salad spinner; any moisture will dilute the dressing. After spinning, the greens can be kept in a perforated plastic bag in the refrigerator for a day or two until ready to use.

When we think of the dressing for a salad an old saying comes to mind. It goes like this: "It takes four people to make the salad properly. A miser to put in the vinegar, a spendthrift to add the oil, a wise man to season the salad, and a madman to toss it!"

The classic choice for the green salad is the old standby dressing of oil, vinegar or lemon juice, salt, and pepper, designed to accent the flavor of the greens while adding just a little sting. Use 4 to 5 parts oil to 1 part vinegar. Cider vinegar and wine vinegar have good flavor and olive oil and salad oil mixed in equal amounts makes a good blend. Use only enough dressing to give the leaves a thin coat or gloss. Approximately ½ cup of dressing will be sufficient for 4 cups of greens.

# BEAN SPROUTS

In 1973 we began to grow alfalfa bean sprouts for salads and mung bean sprouts for my Chinese recipes. They are also sold year round in health-food stores and many supermarkets. The sprouts contribute crispness and a faintly nutty tang to a dish.

In a clean 1-quart jar, soak 1 tablespoon of mung beans in water for 24 hours. Do not use the jar top; instead cover with a double thickness of cheesecloth secured tightly with a rubber band around the top of the jar. After 24 hours drain all of the water off the beans. Now rinse the beans with water 2 or 3 times a day. It is not necessary to remove the cheesecloth when rinsing.

Keep the jar away from the light or in a brown paper bag; the seeds need darkness to sprout. In about five or six days you will have fresh, young, tender bean sprouts. The same process is used for growing the alfalfa seeds.

# CHICKEN SALAD

1 3-lb. chicken, raw
1 rib celery, quartered
1 medium onion, quartered
1 tsp. salt
1 cup finely chopped celery
½ cup sliced, toasted almonds
1 cup mayonnaise

1 tbsp. lemon juice
lettuce leaves for six servings
3 hard-cooked eggs (garnish)
fresh fruit in season (garnish)

*Place the chicken, celery, onion, and salt in a large pot. Add enough water to cover. Bring the water to a boil, then reduce the heat to a low boil, cover the pot, and cook for 20 minutes. Keep the pot covered for 1 hour. (The chicken will be cooked and juicy when prepared in this manner.) At the end of the hour remove the chicken, and when it is cool enough to touch, remove the skin and bones. (The broth may be used for another recipe.) Cut the chicken in 1-inch pieces.*

Add the celery, almonds, mayonnaise, and lemon juice to the chicken pieces, mix well and chill. Arrange the lettuce on the serving plate and spoon the chicken salad in the center.

Garnish, if desired, with hard-cooked eggs, sliced or quartered, and slices of fresh fruit. Serves six.

# SHRIMP SALAD

3 lbs. raw shrimp
1 onion, chopped
1 lemon, sliced
3 dashes Tabasco
3 ribs celery, finely chopped
4 hard-cooked eggs, finely chopped
1 tbsp. sweet pickle relish
1 tbsp. finely chopped green onion

¾ cup mayonnaise
2 tsp. lemon juice
salt and pepper
avocado or tomato (optional)
paprika (garnish)
lemon wedges (garnish)

Rinse and drain the shrimp. Bring 4 quarts water to a boil in a large pot and add the chopped onion, lemon, and Tabasco. Now add the shrimp and boil for 5 minutes. Add 3 cups cold water to the pot to stop the cooking process. Let the shrimp soak for 30 minutes, then drain and let them stand for another 20 minutes. When the shrimp are cool, remove the heads, peel, and dice them.

Mix together the shrimp, celery, eggs, relish, and green onion. Blend in the mayonnaise and lemon juice and add salt and pepper to taste. Chill one hour. The shrimp salad may be served on lettuce or in half of an avocado or half of a tomato. Garnish with a dash of paprika and a wedge of lemon. Serves four to six.

# AVOCADO STUFFED WITH CRABMEAT

*To prepare the dressing:*

1 cup mayonnaise
2 tsp. lemon juice
2 tbsp. capers, drained
3 tbsp. chili sauce

2 tbsp. minced green onions
¼ tsp. black pepper
1 tbsp. minced fresh parsley

*Mix all the ingredients for the dressing together. Refrigerate. Yield: 1½ cups.*

*To assemble the salad:*

3 avocados
juice of 1 lemon
1 lb. lump crabmeat
(remove all shells)

1 head iceberg or Romaine
lettuce

*Halve and peel the avocados, then sprinkle them with lemon juice. Wash the lettuce and pat dry with paper towels. Put the leaves on salad plates, then place half of an avocado on each plate. Fill the halves with crabmeat. Serve the dressing on the side or ladle it over each avocado. Serves six.*

# CAULIFLOWER SALAD

1 medium head cauliflower
½ cup oil (half olive oil and
half vegetable oil is a good
blend)

2 tbsp. vinegar
½ tsp. salt
¼ tsp. pepper
dash Tabasco

*Cut the tough outer leaves and stalks off the cauliflower. Break the cauliflower into flowerets and wash them thoroughly under cold water. Drain. Steam for 5 minutes or until the flowerets are tender-crisp. This means that it is tender for the fork to pierce, but it will still* hold its shape or form. You do not want it to be soft and mushy. Remove the cauliflower from the pot and cool.

Make the dressing by combining the remaining ingredients Pour over the cauliflower and toss lightly. Serves six.

## SLICED CREOLE TOMATOES WITH FRESH SWEET BASIL

3 Creole or any ripe
tomatoes
Leon's Vinaigrette Dressing
(recipe follows)

¼ cup fresh sweet basil,
finely chopped

Place the tomatoes on a large platter in a single layer. Ladle the dressing over each slice, then sprinkle generously with chopped basil. Chill until ready to serve. Serves six.

## LEON'S VINAIGRETTE DRESSING

6 tbsp. olive oil (or 3 tbsp.
olive oil and 3 tbsp.
vegetable oil)
2 tbsp. wine vinegar

½ tsp. salt
¼ tsp. freshly ground black
pepper

Stir all ingredients well. Do not use an electric mixer, because it will emulsify the mixture. Yield: ½ cup.

## SUMMER SALAD

3 large Creole or any ripe
tomatoes, sliced
2 small cucumbers, sliced

1 medium onion, thinly
sliced

For a fresh-from-the-garden taste, combine the ingredients, and serve with an oil-and-vinegar dressing. Serves four to six.

# AVOCADO AND GRAPEFRUIT SALAD

3 avocados
1-qt. can grapefruit
  sections, drained, or 3
  small to medium fresh
  grapefruit, peeled and
  sectioned

1 head Romaine lettuce
1 cup Poppy Seed Dressing
  (recipe follows)

*Cut the avocados in half lengthwise and peel. Slice them in lengthwise pieces, at least 4 slices from each half avocado.*

*Arrange a layer of Romaine lettuce on each plate. Create a spiral effect by alternating slices of avocado and grapefruit. Spoon the dressing over the slices.*

*This is a small salad to be used as a sorbet to refresh the palate between courses during an extended meal. Serves six.*

# POPPY SEED DRESSING

1 cup sugar
2 tsp. dry mustard
1 tsp. salt
⅔ cup cider vinegar

3 tbsp. onion juice
2 cups salad oil (not olive
  oil)
3 tbsp. poppy seeds

*Mix the sugar, mustard, salt and vinegar. Add the onion juice and stir thoroughly. Slowly add the oil, beating constantly with a whisk. Continue to beat until dressing is thick. Then add the poppy seeds and beat a few minutes more. Chill. Yield: 3 ½ cups.*

*Delicious on fruit salads.*

# BING CHERRY SALAD

1 6-oz. package cherry
   gelatin
8 oz. cream cheese
1 17-oz. can dark sweet
   cherries, pitted (reserve
   liquid)

2 cups boiling water
1 cup chopped pecans
Salad oil

*Blend the gelatin and cream cheese in a blender. Drain the cherries, reserving the juice. Chop the berries coarsely. Pour the boiling water over the cream cheese mixture in the blender, then blend well. Add 1 ½ cups cherry liquid, the cherries, and the pecans. Lightly brush a 3-cup mold with salad oil, then pour the cherry mixture into the mold. Let chill in the refrigerator for one hour, then stir and continue chilling for 2 hours until firm. Serves eight to ten.*

# FRESH FRUIT SALAD

2 apples
lemon juice
2 oranges
1 small pink grapefruit
1 banana, cut in ½-inch
   pieces

1 pint whole strawberries
1 head Romaine lettuce
Honey dressing

*Peel and slice the apples and sprinkle them with a little lemon juice to prevent them from turning brown. Peel the oranges and the grapefruit, cutting them in sections and removing all of the membranes. Peel and slice the banana. Arrange the fruit in a spiral design on the lettuce using the banana as the hub or center. Place the whole strawberries on top of the banana pieces. Spoon HONEY DRESSING over the fruit. Serves six.*

# HONEY DRESSING

½ cup honey                                    ⅛ tsp. ground ginger
½ cup fresh lime juice

    *Combine the ingredients and stir well. Serve on fruit salad. Yield:*
*1 cup.*

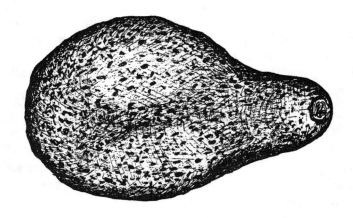

*sauces & seasonings*

The Creoles are famous for their splendid sauces; they know that sauces are the glory of French cuisine, and so they use them with great delight. The successful making of a good sauce is a necessity. A sauce is added to perk up the taste of a certain food or to add piquancy; sometimes to contrast and then again to complement the main ingredient. The number of sauces open to a Creole chef are endless and to name even half of them would be a tremendous task. Therefore, I have chosen a few of the more popular sauces and will explain the best way to serve and enjoy them.

Leon was quite young when he became aware of the value of sauces. Leon would often help his mother with the cooking. When he was about eleven years old his mother was ill, and so Leon prepared an oyster soup and some codfish balls for supper one evening. He put the plate of codfish balls on top of the pot of oyster soup. Just before it was time for his father to arrive home, Leon rushed in from playing to warm the soup. He accidentally tipped the plate and the codfish balls fell into the pot of soup. He was a bit shocked at the disaster; he knew his father to be a very particular person. Perhaps he would not like the "new dish." But Leon, being a very innovative type, declared that he had created something different. Much to his surprise his father ate heartily, and pronounced the supper different, but delicious. Leon was elated; he always believed that was the moment he decided that he could cook. The serendipity of Leon's accidental discovery was that he learned how well the oyster flavor complemented the codfish. And so it is with our sauces. When we combine Béchamel Sauce with sautéed and seasoned shrimp it becomes Shrimp Yvette (see index).

Rich sauces should be used sparingly and with discretion. A sauce is chosen to enhance the flavor of the food it accompanies, not to overwhelm it. The addition of a delectable sauce changes the very nature of a dish. Poached eggs, for example, are nutritious and just what you may wish for an everyday breakfast. But add Hollandaise Sauce, along with a bit of fried ham or Canadian bacon and an English muffin, and voilà—you now have an elegant entrée: Eggs Benedict!

One of the most flavorful of the Creole sauces is the peppery Sauce Piquante. It can be used with turtle meat, shrimp, crawfish,

fish, and wild and domestic birds and is the sauce called for in the recipe for Chicken Carnival (see index).

It has been said that Creole cooking almost always begins with "First, you make a roux . . ." and this is true. The best-tasting Creole specialties begin with this directive. You may think that making a roux sounds mysterious or difficult, but it really is not. See "How To Make a Roux" in this chapter and you will soon master this most important basic Creole skill.

## ANITA'S MORNAY SAUCE

3 tbsp. butter
2 tsp. finely chopped green
  onions (remove tops)
3 tbsp. flour
⅔ cup water or stock (either
  chicken or seafood)
⅓ cup vermouth

2 egg yolks
1 cup cream
pinch nutmeg
⅛ tsp. cayenne pepper
pinch salt
¼ cup Swiss or Gruyère
  cheese

*In a heavy-bottomed saucepan, melt the butter over moderate heat. When it foams, add the onions and sauté one minute; add the flour. Stir constantly. Cook over low heat until bubbly (do not brown) and slowly add the water or stock and vermouth, blending well. Simmer for 5 minutes, then remove from the heat and set aside.*

*In a bowl add the egg yolks and the cream; beat together until blended. Add the nutmeg, cayenne pepper, and salt. Add ½ cup of the vermouth mixture to the egg yolks and cream, stirring constantly. Now add this mixture into the pan with the sauce. Over low heat, cook, stirring constantly with a wire whisk until the sauce thickens and is well heated. Now add the cheese. Continue stirring to keep the sauce smooth while it thickens (about 3 minutes). Serve immediately. Yield: about 1¾ cups.*

*Note: This sauce is excellent on fish, shrimp, egg, and vegetable dishes.*

# AMANDINE SAUCE

This is basically the same sauce as the Meunière, except that Worcestershire sauce and almonds are added.

**2 sticks butter**
**1 cup slivered almonds**
**juice of 2 lemons**
**2 tbsp. Worcestershire**
  **sauce**

**3 tbsp. finely minced fresh**
  **parsley**

*In a heavy saucepan, melt the butter over low heat, then add the almonds to the skillet and cook over low heat until they are a light golden brown. Remove the pan from the heat and add the lemon juice, Worcestershire sauce, and the parsley. Stir; the lemon juice will make the sauce foam. When the foaming subsides, return the pan to low heat for about 1 minute. Stir to mix, and your sauce is ready. Yield: about 1½ cups.*

# MEUNIÈRE SAUCE

**2 sticks butter**
**1 tsp. freshly ground black**
  **pepper**

**juice of 2 lemons**
**3 tbsp. finely minced fresh**
  **parsley**

*In a heavy saucepan melt the butter slowly over low heat, then cook over low heat until the butter begins to turn a golden straw color (do not brown). Remove the pan from the heat and add the pepper, the lemon juice, and the parsley. Stir; the lemon juice will make the sauce foam. When the foaming subsides, return the pan to low heat for about 1 minute. Stir to mix, and your sauce is ready. Yield: about 1 cup.*

*Note: This butter sauce is one of our most popular and versatile sauces. If you are pan-frying fish or crabs, use the same pan in which you sauté the seafood. The brown residue in the bottom of the pan should be scraped loose and used in the sauce.*

# BÉCHAMEL SAUCE

This sauce, actually made with milk, is used for creaming foods like vegetables and fish and as a base for other sauces. It can be used to stretch leftovers and gives cooked foods an entirely new life. The foolproof way to attain a perfectly smooth sauce is to make sure your milk is hot when you add it to the butter and flour.

| | |
|---|---|
| **2 tbsp. butter or margarine** | **½ tsp. salt** |
| **2 tbsp. flour** | **¼ tsp. pepper** |
| **1 cup milk, heated** | |

*Melt the butter in a heavy saucepan. Stir in the flour and cook over a low to medium heat, stirring constantly, until the paste bubbles a bit—but do not let it brown. This process should take about 2 minutes. Add the hot milk, continuing to stir as the sauce thickens. Bring to a gentle boil, add the salt and pepper to taste, lower the heat and simmer, stirring for 2 to 3 minutes more. Remove from the heat. You may cool this sauce for later use; in that case, cover it with plastic wrap. Yield: 1 cup.*

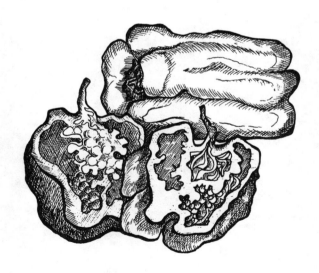

# HOLLANDAISE SAUCE

3 egg yolks
dash Tabasco or pinch
  cayenne pepper
¼ tsp. salt

1 tbsp. boiling water
1 stick unsalted butter,
  melted
1 tbsp. warm lemon juice

*Put the egg yolks, Tabasco or cayenne pepper, and salt in a 1-quart heavy saucepan over very low heat or in the top of a double boiler over, but not touching, hot water. Beat the yolks with a wire whisk until the they begin to thicken. Now, add the tablespoon of boiling water. Beat again until the egg yolks have thickened to the consistency of heavy cream. If the egg yolks are not beaten to this stage, they will not be able to absorb and hold the butter as they should, and the sauce will not thicken properly.*

*Slowly whisk the warm, not hot, melted butter a small amount at a time until the sauce begins to thicken into a very heavy cream. Beating constantly, whisk in all the butter. When the sauce is thick enough to coat the whisk, beat in the warm lemon juice. Remove the double boiler from the heat. Serve at once. Yield: 1 cup.*

*Note: This sauce is called for in the recipe for Eggs Sardou (see index).*

# BLENDER HOLLANDAISE

This is virtually a no-fail method if the butter is hot when added.

**3 egg yolks (room
temperature)**
**2 tbsp. lemon juice**
**⅛ tsp. salt**

**¼ tsp. Tabasco or dash
cayenne pepper**
**1 stick butter, melted and
hot**

*Put the egg yolks, lemon juice, and seasonings into a blender; blend just until the eggs are foamy, about 5 seconds. Heat the butter in a saucepan until it foams, but do not let it brown. Remove the insert from the cover of the blender (leave the cover on to prevent spattering) and, with the machine running, pour in the bubbling hot butter in a thin steady stream. It will thicken very quickly, in a matter of seconds rather than minutes. If the sauce is too thick, stir in 1 to 2 tablespoons of hot water. Taste and correct the seasonings. Yield: about ¾ cup.*

# BROWN GRAVY

**2 qts. beef stock**
**3 tbsp. butter**

**3 tbsp. flour**

*Place the beef stock in a large saucepan and, on a simmer, reduce to approximately 1 quart. This will take about 2 hours. Then melt the butter in a heavy saucepan, add the flour, and cook over low heat, stirring constantly to keep it smooth until the flour is a golden brown. Slowly add the stock and stir until well blended. Bring to a boil and then reduce the heat; simmer for about 20 minutes, stirring frequently. Yield: 3 cups.*

# CREOLE SAUCE

2 tbsp. butter
1 cup coarsely chopped
onions
1 cup finely chopped green
pepper
½ cup finely chopped celery
2 cloves garlic, minced
1 tsp. minced fresh parsley
½ bay leaf
¼ tsp. thyme
¼ tsp. cayenne pepper

1 tsp. brown sugar
2 tsp. paprika
2 cups diced tomatoes,
fresh or canned
½ cup chili sauce
½ cup tomato juice
1 tbsp. Worcestershire
sauce
1 tbsp. Tabasco
4 tsp. cornstarch
⅓ cup water

*Melt the butter in a Dutch oven and sauté the onions, green pepper, celery, garlic, and parsley over moderate heat. When the onions become soft add the remaining ingredients except the cornstarch and water and stir well. Simmer until the sauce is reduced by about one-third, stirring constantly.*

*Combine the cornstarch and water and stir into the sauce. Simmer over moderate heat, stirring constantly, until the sauce has thickened, about 1½ minutes. This sauce tastes even better the next day. Yield: 2 cups.*

# BÉARNAISE SAUCE

juice of 1 lemon
1½ tsp. Worcestershire
sauce
⅛ tsp. cayenne pepper
¼ tsp. salt
1 tbsp. tarragon vinegar
3 tsp. dried tarragon leaves

4 egg yolks (room
temperature)
2 tbsp. dry white wine
1 stick cold butter plus 1
stick melted butter
pinch white pepper

*Place the lemon juice, Worcestershire sauce, cayenne pepper, salt, tarragon vinegar, and 2 teaspoons of the tarragon leaves into a* glass or enamel saucepan. Boil until reduced to 2 tablespoons. Strain and set aside.

Place the egg yolks and the wine in the top of a double boiler over barely simmering water. With a wire whisk beat the egg mixture until it is slightly thickened, approximately 3 or 4 minutes. Add the cold butter, small pieces at a time, whisking all the while. Now add the melted butter a droplet or two at a time, whisking constantly until all has been added. Whisk in the reserved lemon juice–tarragon mixture, add a pinch of white pepper, and the remaining teaspoon of the tarragon leaves. Mix well. Yield: 1 ½ cups.

## CHORON SAUCE

**1 part Creole Sauce**    **1 part Béarnaise Sauce**

In a heavy saucepan, reduce the Creole Sauce by about one-fourth. Add the Béarnaise Sauce and stir until well blended.

## EGG SAUCE

**½ stick butter**
**6 green onions, minced**
**4 tbsp. flour**
**2 ½ cups fish stock, heated**
**salt and black pepper to**
**    taste**

**2 tbsp. dry white wine**
**2 drops Tabasco**
**2 hard-cooked eggs, very**
**    finely chopped**

Melt the butter in a heavy skillet over very low heat. Add the green onions and sauté for about 5 minutes. Add the flour, mix well, and cook over very low heat stirring constantly for 4 to 5 minutes more. Slowly over low heat add the hot stock stirring until it is well mixed. Raise the heat and allow this mixture to come to a boil, then turn the heat to low and let it simmer for 5 minutes. Add the salt and pepper, wine, and Tabasco. Mix well and taste. Add the chopped eggs, mix into the sauce and serve immediately. Yield: about 2 cups.

# LEMON SAUCE

½ cup sugar
1 tbsp. cornstarch
1 cup water

2 tbsp. butter
1 tbsp. lemon rind
3 tbsp. lemon juice

*Combine the sugar and cornstarch in a saucepan and add the water. Over moderate heat, stirring constantly, bring the water to a low boil. When the sugar is dissolved, reduce the heat and simmer slowly, stirring constantly until the mixture thickens and becomes clear.*

*Remove from the heat and add the remaining ingredients.*

*Serve hot or cold on cakes, puddings, or pancakes. Yield: about 1 ½ cups.*

*Note: Try this sauce on my Banana-Pecan Pancakes (see index).*

# SAUCE PIQUANTE

2 tbsp. butter
2 tbsp. oil
1½ cups finely chopped
   onions
1 cup chopped green onions
1 cup finely chopped celery
1 cup finely chopped bell
   pepper
4 tbsp. flour
1 16-oz. can tomatoes
1 6-oz. can tomato paste
2 cups chicken stock
1½ cups water

4 cloves garlic, finely
   chopped
1 lemon, thinly sliced
¼ tsp. cayenne pepper
½ tsp. black pepper
1 tsp. salt
1 tsp. basil
½ tsp. thyme
1 tsp. chili powder
4 bay leaves
1 tbsp. finely chopped fresh
   parsley

*Heat the butter and oil in a heavy saucepan. When the butter has melted and begins to simmer, add the onions, green onions, celery,* and bell pepper and cook over moderate heat. Sauté slowly until the vegetables begin to change color and become transparent. Sprinkle in the flour and mix well. Cook over low heat, stirring constantly for about 5 minutes. Add the tomatoes and tomato paste and cook 5 minutes longer. Pour in the stock and water, mixing well. As this mixture slowly simmers, add the garlic, lemon, cayenne pepper, black pepper, salt, basil, thyme, chili powder, and bay leaves. Simmer for about ½ hour, then add the parsley. Yield: 3 cups.

Note: Piquante means pungent; the sauce should be distinctly peppery. Louisiana cooks use Sauce Piquante with turtle meat, shrimp, crawfish, fish, and wild or domestic birds of every kind.

# WHITE SAUCE

White Sauce is truly a valuable basic ingredient. It can be used as a base for sauces, for vegetables, eggs, poultry, meat, creamed or gratinéed dishes, seafood, and crepes.

| Thin | Medium | Thick |
|------|--------|-------|
| 1 tbsp. butter | 2 tbsp. butter | 4 tbsp. butter |
| 1 tbsp. flour | 2 tbsp. flour | 4 tbsp. flour |
| 1 cup milk | 1 cup milk | 1 cup milk |
| ¼ tsp. salt | ¼ tsp. salt | ¼ tsp. salt |
| ⅛ tsp. white pepper | ⅛ tsp. white pepper | ⅛ tsp. white pepper |

Melt the butter over medium-low heat in a heavy-bottomed saucepan. Stir in the flour and blend thoroughly, stirring constantly. Do not allow to brown. Cook for 2 to 3 minutes. Gradually add the milk and stir in the seasonings. Reduce heat to low and beat vigorously with a wire whisk until the sauce is thick and smooth. Yield: 1 cup.

# HOW TO MAKE A ROUX

The first thing you need to make a roux is a heavy pot. Next, have your vegetables chopped and ready and heat the water or stock that you intend to add. The amount of liquid depends on what you are preparing.

Use equal amounts of flour and fat (oil, lard, or butter). Start by heating, for example, 3 tablespoons of fat over low heat, then add the 3 tablespoons of flour all at one time into the pot, stirring constantly. Gently blend this mixture of flour and fat over low heat from 5 minutes for a white roux to 30 or 40 minutes for a dark, reddish-brown roux. As you stir the roux constantly you will see the color change before your eyes—from white to barely blond, on to beige, then brown like peanut butter, then to hazel-nut brown, and finally to a dark, reddish-brown. You must watch very carefully and stir constantly because you do not want the flour to burn. If it does, throw it out and start all over again because the burned flour will give a very bitter taste. (Remember that a heavy pot retains heat, so you may want to remove the pot temporarily from the fire, for a few minutes, just before you reach the desired color.) You want to cook the roux long enough to avoid the raw taste of flour. Therefore, you can't rush the process and achieve the desired taste.

The best way to stop the roux from continuing to cook when it is the desired rich, brown color is to add the chopped onion, bell pepper, and celery all at once. Now inhale and enjoy the appetizing aroma! When the vegetables are cooked to your preference, add the hot stock or water, and mix thoroughly.

Then you may increase the heat when you add the balance of the ingredients for your gumbo or stew.

The white roux takes about 5 minutes to make. In a saucepan, melt 2 tablespoons of butter, for example, over medium-low heat. Blend in 2 tablespoons of flour, and cook slowly, stirring constantly. Do not allow to brown. Cook for about 2 minutes; remove from the heat. Pour in one cup of hot liquid—stock, water, or milk—all at once and whisk vigorously to blend well. On low heat cook and beat vigorously with a wire whisk until the sauce is thick and smooth.

The white roux is called for in making a White Sauce, Bechamel Sauce, and again, when you make Oyster Soup (see index).

# HERBS AND SPICES

Preserving the natural flavor of food is a top priority for any cook. We do not wish to overpower that flavor, which is often quite subtle, so we need to have a light hand in the use of herbs and spices. Nevertheless, herbs are indispensable if you wish to capture the real flavor and fragrance of Creole cooking.

When the Ursuline nuns came to New Orleans in the early 1700s to care for the sick in the Hospital of New Orleans, they immediately requested a cleared area of the yard for an herb garden. Herbs were used medicinally, as well as in many teas (such as mint or dandelion) and liqueurs (such as anisette and absinthe). Herbal teas are still popular today.

The full fragrance of herbs comes mainly from the volatile oils released when the *fresh* leaves are chopped, pounded, or fried in oil. Oil is a wonderful carrier of flavors.

Creole food is universally known as flavorful and spicy. Many of our most popular spices—bay leaf, basil, thyme, black pepper, cayenne, allspice, cloves, poultry seasoning, chili powder, curry, and filé powder—are discussed in *La Bouche Creole*.

Here are some additional, often-used herbs and spices.

## ANISE

We use anise in some of our oyster appetizers. Anise is available as an extract or in seed form. It is the principal ingredient in absinthe, a liqueur used to make the Absinthe Frappé, one of our popular cocktails. In early Creole days most of the families made their own anisette, a sweet liqueur. Anise is also used in coffee cakes, sweet rolls, cookies, and sweet pickles. It has a licorice flavor.

## CARDAMON

This is available ground or as little dried pods. Within the pod are the tiny brown seeds that we use in coffee cakes, buns, some pastries, cookies, stewed fruit, and grape jelly.

## CHIVES

A popular plant and found in most herb gardens, chives are in the onion family and grow like green onions with slender green tops. They have a delicate onion flavor. We mince them and add them to salads and vegetables, meat and poultry dishes, and eggs.

## CINNAMON

Cinnamon is one of our most often-used spices. It comes from the aromatic bark of the cinnamon tree. We use it in stick form for hot wine punch in the winter and sometimes in spiced coffee or cider. We also use it in pickling and canning our spiced pears and brandied peaches. We use ground cinnamon in cooking fruits especially, and in baking puddings, pies, spice cakes, and the ever-popular cinnamon toast.

## DILL

Dill is another herb grown in our gardens. It's a member of the parsley family. We use dill to flavor vinegar and in pickling. It's also good to flavor potatoes, sauerkraut, cauliflower, and green apple pie. We like it on garlic bread and, mixed with butter, it's good for basting fish.

## GINGER

This is the pungent-flavored root of a plant grown in China and Japan. It is a strange-looking, gnarled chunk of root. Ginger tastes best thinly sliced and sautéed in hot oil to extract the flavor. Then any food sautéed in the oil will be impregnated with the exotic taste of the ginger. When it is ground, it is valuable for flavoring baked items, such as gingerbread and pumpkin pie.

## MARJORAM

Sweet marjoram, a member of the mint family, is very fragrant. We grow this easily in our herb garden and use it frequently in our stews and gravies. It's also good in beans and in lamb dishes.

## NUTMEG

This is an excellent spice. It can be overpowering so it requires a light hand. We can purchase it ground, but I prefer to get the whole nutmeg, which is a hard seed imported from the East and West Indies. We take the whole nutmeg and grate a small amount into rice pudding, calas (rice cakes), custards, and quiches. We use it with vegetables and in sauces and in some seafood dishes. It's also a "must" for hot wine drinks and eggnog.

## OREGANO

Oregano has a strong aromatic flavor. This pungent herb, another member of the mint family, is an important component in many marinades and is traditionally used in tomato dishes, especially Italian spaghetti sauce. It is essential for flavoring pizza, and is also good in pork dishes.

## ROSEMARY

Rosemary is a beautiful and aromatic herb. It has pinkish foliage and can be used decoratively. This herb is very good with lamb, roast beef, and beef stew. It is also good in green salad and with cooked vegetables such as potatoes, green beans, and cauliflower.

## SAGE

This is an old favorite herb for flavoring stuffings and sausages. With baked chicken or duck it is very pleasant. It also goes well with pork.

## TARRAGON

This is a delightful herb used for flavoring tarragon vinegar, tomato dishes, chicken, and meat. We use tarragon in our Béarnaise Sauce, and it is also excellent in salad dressings and fish sauces.

## WHITE PEPPER

These peppers are the small dried berry of a vine native to the East Indies. White pepper is made from the fully ripened berry after the dark outer shell has been buffed away. The berry is then ground. White pepper is milder than black pepper and is especially nice to use in white sauces or light foods when specks of black pepper would be unattractive. Grind your own pepper for a fresher flavor.

# FLAVORINGS

## LEMONS

In Creole cuisine we use a great deal of lemon. It is a very versatile fruit and is piquant and invigorating. A combination of its juice and the essence of the rind is used in numerous ways, from soup to dessert. Its special taste and fragrance gives Sauce Piquante its piquancy. Lemons are also essential to our boiled seafood.

## VANILLA EXTRACT

An extract is a preparation containing a flavoring in a concentrated form. The preparation contains the essential oils of the product with alcohol added.

We keep a vanilla bean in the sugar canister. The fragrance is divine. Also, in making homemade vanilla ice cream, we scald half the milk with a half-inch piece of vanilla bean for extra flavor and fragrance. After the bean has been in milk for 20 minutes, remove the bean and split it into two pieces, then scrape it well and add the pulp to the milk. Wash and dry the hull of the bean and place it in your sugar bowl.

This popular flavoring is called for in most of our puddings, cakes and other desserts.

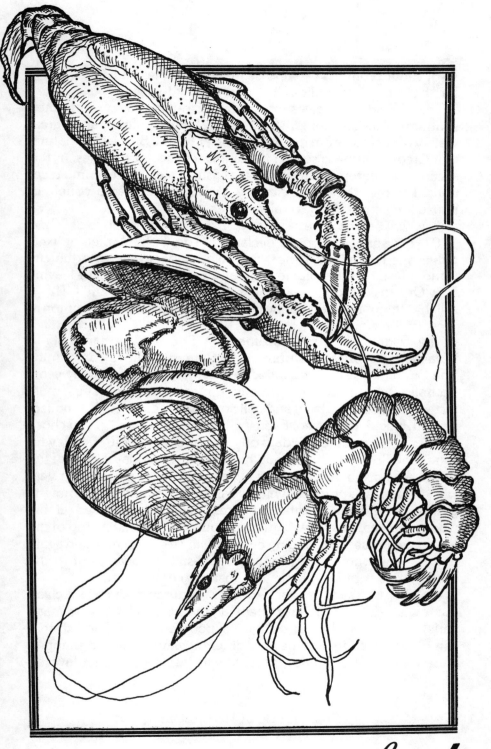

seafood

It should come as no surprise that the Creoles had a great liking for "fruits de la mer," literally, "the fruits of the sea."

They found themselves practically surrounded by water in their southern Louisiana home. They had an abundant supply and a great variety of seafood from this water all year round. So it is only natural that Creole cuisine is so rich in magnificent seafood dishes. In this section I've featured fish, crabs, crawfish, oysters, and shrimp creations. For the more stout-hearted, I've also included a couple of unusual recipes calling for alligator.

New Orleanians have always been known for their love of fish. A 1901 newspaper clipping declares: "The Fish Market of New Orleans is famous over the world. No stranger comes to the city without visiting this notable spot, and one never thinks of leaving New Orleans without enjoying a 'Fish Dinner' at West End." This is still the "thing" to do on Friday night, when long lines are common at West End restaurants.

The tradition of eating seafood on Friday night came about because New Orleans is primarily a Roman Catholic community. The Church has since rescinded the restriction, but for many years Catholics had to abstain from eating meat on Friday. Thus, most restaurants featured tasty and delicious seafood, which they boiled, broiled, baked, or stewed. Even if you were not Catholic, you chose seafood restaurants on Fridays out of deference to your friends who were. The Friday night seafood habit continues today. Some of the restaurants are built on pilings over Lake Pontchartrain with very wide verandas or porches, which were once screened but are now all glassed-in and air-conditioned. Fresh seafood is served at big wooden tables. The view is great as you sit practically on top of the lake watching sea gulls gliding by and diving for a fish now and again and the sailboats drifting by with their sails billowing out in the breeze. This is pure esthetic and gustatory enjoyment!

Whether we savor the good food of restaurants, catch and clean our own fish, or purchase them at the seafood market, many varieties are available for culinary experimentation. One fish that can be prepared in a number of different ways is the red snapper. Here we offer a recipe for it served with pecans. Another favored local fish is catfish. When it is dipped in cornmeal and fried crisply to perfection, it can tempt the most discriminating fish lover. Then there's the ever-popular stuffed flounder, another delightful dish.

A place of great significance is held for the most delectable and delicious bivalve—the oyster. Louisiana oysters are eagerly sought and highly prized for their exquisite flavor and unsurpassed quality. We eat them raw, on the half-shell, and in many exceptionally palatable dishes.

And then last but not least is "M'sieu le mud bug," as Leon was wont to call the crawfish. This was his favorite of favorites. Try the recipe for Crawfish Pie—I'm sure you'll like it.

As they have been since early Creole times, "fruits de la mer" continue to be one of our most important and popular food specialties. I hope that some of these New Orleans favorites will become yours too.

# REDFISH WITH OYSTER SAUCE

1 stick butter
4 green onions, finely
  chopped
¼ cup finely chopped celery
2 cloves garlic, minced
2 tbsp. minced parsley
1 tbsp. flour
¾ cup oyster liquor

4 tbsp. dry white wine
½ cup whipping cream
16 freshly shucked raw
  oysters
4 6-oz. redfish fillets
salt and black pepper to
  taste
paprika

*Melt half of the butter in a skillet over low heat, then sauté the green onions, celery, garlic, and half of the parsley until the celery is soft. Now add the flour and mix well, then add the oyster liquor and the wine and simmer over low heat, stirring constantly, for 3 or 4 minutes until the sauce thickens and reduces a little. Add the cream, stir well, and simmer for 2 or 3 minutes more until the sauce is well blended. Add the oysters and cook for 5 minutes. Cover the sauce and set it aside, but keep it warm.*

*Melt the remaining butter and generously brush the fillets with the melted butter; sprinkle the fish with salt, pepper, and Tabasco. Put the balance of the butter and the seasoned fillets in a broiler pan and broil them 4 to 5 minutes on each side or until the fish flakes easily.*

*To serve, pour the oyster sauce over the fish, and sprinkle with the rest of the parsley and a little paprika. Serve hot. Serves four.*

# RED SNAPPER WITH PECANS

4 6- to 8-oz. red snapper
   fillets
2 cups milk
½ tsp. salt
½ tsp. pepper
¼ tsp. cayenne pepper
1 cup flour

2 tbsp. margarine
2 tbsp. vegetable oil
2 tbsp. butter
½ cup chopped pecans
2 tbsp. Worcestershire
   sauce
3 tbsp. lemon juice

*Place the fish fillets in the milk and marinate in the refrigerator for 30 minutes.*

*Remove the fillets, drain well, and dry them with paper towels. Mix the salt, and black and cayenne pepper together. Sprinkle the fillets lightly with salt-and-pepper mixture and then dust them with flour.*

*Heat the margarine and oil in a heavy skillet, and over medium heat lightly brown the fillets on each side.*

*Place the cooked fish on a warm serving dish. Now add the butter to the skillet. Add the pecans to the skillet and cook for 3 or 4 minutes, over low heat, stirring constantly until the pecans are golden; add the Worcestershire sauce and the lemon juice. Stir well and pour over the fillets and serve immediately. Serves four.*

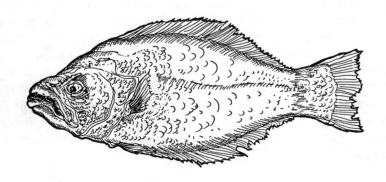

# TROUT LEON

6 6- to 8-oz. trout fillets
1 cup cold milk
salt and black pepper
½ lb. sliced fresh
  mushrooms
1 stick melted butter plus 2
  tbsp. butter
2 egg yolks
¼ cup finely chopped green
  onions

2 tbsp. flour
1 cup scalded milk
¼ cup dry white wine
¼ tsp. white pepper
dash Tabasco
1 cup whipping cream,
  whipped
dash freshly ground nutmeg

*Marinate the trout fillets in the cold milk for ½ hour in the refrigerator. Remove the fillets from the milk, pat dry, sprinkle with salt and pepper, and arrange them in a baking dish. Add the mushrooms to the baking pan and pour half of the melted butter on top. Preheat the oven to 350 degrees and bake until the fish flakes, about 15 to 20 minutes.*

*While the fish is baking, prepare the sauce. Place the egg yolks in a mixing bowl and beat with a whisk until they have thickened. Now beat in the remaining ½ cup butter, a little at a time. Set aside.*

*In a saucepan or skillet place the 2 tablespoons of butter and over low heat sauté the green onions. Do not brown. When the onions are soft, add the flour and mix well. Simmer about 4 minutes over low heat, stirring constantly. Slowly add the scalded milk, stirring all the time. Let this sauce cook until thickened, about 4 or 5 minutes. Remove from the heat and when the sauce is almost cool, stir in the egg yolks and butter and mix well. Add the wine, white pepper, and Tabasco.*

*When the fish is cooked, remove it from the oven and preheat the broiler. Now fold the whipping cream into the sauce, add the nutmeg, and spoon it over the fish. Brown slightly under the broiler, watching very carefully so that it does not burn. Serve immediately. Serves four to six.*

# FRIED CATFISH

2 medium-sized (about 1
   lb.) catfish, tenderloined,
   skinless, and cut into 3-
   inch pieces *or* 4 catfish
   fillets, cut into 3-inch
   pieces
cold milk (enough to cover
   the fillets in a bowl)

1½ tsp. salt
1 tsp. black pepper
1 tsp. cayenne pepper
1½ cups yellow cornmeal
1 cup vegetable oil

*Rinse the catfish quickly under cold running water. Put them in a bowl and add the cold milk to cover them; marinate them in the refrigerator for at least 30 minutes.*

*Mix the salt, the black pepper, and ½ tsp. cayenne pepper together. Combine the cornmeal and the remaining ½ tsp. of cayenne pepper.*

*Preheat the oil in a deep fryer to 365 degrees.*

*Lift the fish out of the milk and pat completely dry with paper towels. Season the fillets on both sides with the salt and pepper mixture; roll in the cornmeal.*

*Deep-fry. It is important to keep the oil at 365 degrees to fry the fish properly. Don't overcrowd the pan. This can be done with 2 or 3 pieces at a time for 6 to 8 minutes or until golden brown. Fish cooks quickly, so by the time it is golden brown on both sides, it is fully cooked. Drain on a paper towel–lined platter and keep warm in a preheated 200-degree oven until ready to serve. Serves four.*

# FRIED ALLIGATOR FILLETS

8 ¼-inch-thick alligator
  fillets
1 cup buttermilk
dash salt
2 eggs, well beaten

½ tsp. black pepper
3 drops Tabasco
1 cup Italian bread crumbs
4 tbsp. vegetable oil

*Pound the fillets with the flat end of a cleaver. Soak them in the buttermilk and salt for at least 30 minutes, then drain and pat dry. Beat the eggs; add the pepper and the Tabasco. Dip each fillet in the eggs, and then in the bread crumbs. In a skillet, heat the oil to 360°–375° and brown the fillets on both sides. Drain on paper towels and serve immediately. Serves four.*

# ALLIGATOR SAUCE PIQUANTE

4 lbs. alligator meat
¼ cup oil
2 tbsp. butter
1½ cups finely chopped
  onions
1 cup finely chopped celery
1 cup finely chopped bell
  pepper
½ cup chopped green
  onions plus 1 tbsp.
3 tbsp. minced fresh parsley
  plus 1 tbsp.
4 tbsp. flour
1 16-oz. can tomatoes

1 6-oz. can tomato paste
3 cups chicken stock
1 cup water
4 cloves garlic, finely
  chopped
1 lemon, thinly sliced
¼ tsp. cayenne pepper
¼ tsp. black pepper
1½ tsp. salt
1 tsp. basil
½ tsp. thyme
1 tsp. chili powder
4 bay leaves
cooked rice

*Cut the alligator meat into l-inch cubes; remove all fat because this is what gives the meat a gamy taste. Rinse the alligator very well. Now, brown the meat pieces in a heavy Dutch oven in the oil, then remove them and set aside. Pour out all but 2 tablespoons of*

*oil, add the butter, and when hot add the onions, celery, bell pepper,
½ cup green onions, and 3 tablespoons parsley. Sauté slowly until
the vegetables become transparent. Sprinkle in the flour, mix well,
and simmer for about 5 minutes stirring constantly over low heat.*

*Add the tomatoes and tomato paste and cook 5 minutes longer.
Pour in the chicken stock and water and continue to simmer,
stirring occasionally. Add the garlic, lemon, cayenne pepper, black
pepper, salt, basil, thyme, chili powder, and bay leaves. Simmer for
½ hour, then add the browned alligator meat. Cook on low simmer,
partially covered, for 1½ hours or until tender. Check the meat
carefully; it must not fall apart when served, yet it must be tender
enough to chew pleasantly. When done, add the 1 tablespoon
green onions and the 1 tablespoon parsley. Serve over rice. Serves
six.*

# CRABS

When I think of crabs, it is not only the crabmeat that we use in so
many ways that comes to my mind, but also the fun times that
revolve around seafood.

One of our favorite summertime activities was "crabbing." There
were many trips, but one especially sticks in my mind. My parents,
my sisters, Shirley and Gloria, and I went to Delacroix Island. We had
all of the accessories necessary—all we needed was bright and sunny
weather so the crabs would bite. We had hand lines made from
strong pieces of twine. One end was tied to the chicken necks—our
bait. The other end was looped over the wrist so that we wouldn't
lose the line easily. Popsi, my father, had a scoop net. Now this is a
tricky operation. The crabs ate the bait, and if we were holding the
line, we could feel the line pull, letting us know we had a "bite." We
squealed in youthful delight, "Come quickly, Popsi." Whereupon
Popsi brought the net and lowered it in the water beneath the hand
line. We gently pulled up the line so as not to frighten or lose the crab.
Much to our surprise we sometimes got two crabs. When caught, the
crabs were put in a hamper and covered with a wet burlap sack. We

caught enough crabs to fill the hamper before the sun was very high. What a successful trip that was!

The ritual of boiling the crabs often followed the outings. When the guests arrived, they saw old newspapers lining the table, large platters of crabs, and lots of cold beer and paper napkins. We all settled down to an enjoyable meal and a pleasant evening.

Besides the crabs caught in the bayous, we also get beautiful blue-point crabs from Lake Pontchartrain, which are similar to crabs found in the Chesapeake Bay area, and from all along the Gulf Coast. We have fresh crabmeat available in our seafood markets year round, and we point with pride to the various delightful ways that the New Orleanian has of serving crabmeat, such as Cheese and Crabmeat Casserole, Crab Fricassée, Crab and Shrimp Etouffée, Crab Stew, and Crabmeat-Mushroom Casserole.

## CRAB STEW

When I was in the third grade, one evening my father made the announcement that we would soon be moving! Talk about a bolt from the blue or being speechless or stunned, we were all those things as we listened to the news that the family was now going to own its own home. Papete went on to explain that he had applied for a loan. It had been approved, and in a few short weeks we would be packing up bag and baggage and moving out to Edgewood.

Edgewood? Where was that? Okay, further explanation revealed that our new neighborhood would be in a suburb called Gentilly, east of New Orleans. As we also later discovered, Edgewood was a section of the city that was a little difficult to get to. There was a streetcar that ran out there, but it wasn't just an ordinary streetcar ride. To get to Edgewood proper the car had to run over a viaduct, which was about a mile long. This ride could be a terrifying experience for all but the bravest of souls. In those days, the Gentilly streetcar would make the trip along Franklin Avenue all the way out to Dreaux Avenue, which was the end of the line. I have to explain, though, that every other car, as it proceeded along Franklin Avenue, would stop at Dorgenois Street and then start back, so that only half of the cars ran all the way.

I mentioned the viaduct holding fears for some people. For example, after we had moved, some of our relatives would not brave the streetcar trip and the only way we received visits from them was when they came the long way, out the Old Gentilly Road and down Franklin Avenue. Let me describe the terrifying journey in more detail. The streetcars were the old-time, real Toonerville-trolley types. They were very small by today's standards, with a seating capacity of about fifty. They bounced and swayed a lot. On level ground this wasn't too bad, but when the car was running on the bridgelike structure over the viaduct, it was pretty unnerving. As you looked through the side window, you seemed to be suspended about twenty feet mid-air. It was rather breathtaking! At times it seemed as though the viaduct itself was swaying as the car bounced along. For some, the trip was really a frightening experience that a lot of timid souls were too fearful to attempt.

But I started to relate how Papete finally became a homeowner. It seems that he ran across this bargain, a three-room house on a thirty-foot lot and just half a block from the streetcar line for only fourteen hundred dollars. Imagine, a house and lot for only fourteen hundred dollars! Of course we were all thrilled, and eagerly waited for Sunday, when Papete promised we would take a ride out to see the house. It was early on Sunday morning, right after church, that we all got ready to visit what would ultimately turn out to be a happy home for all of us for many years. Naturally, we were excited. Don't forget, this was at a time when owning a house was not the casual thing it is today. Oh no, the great majority of families were "renters," with only the well-to-do able to own their own homes.

And so we were off to Edgewood. Finally, we arrived at the corner of Bay Street and Franklin Avenue, and the whole family got off the streetcar. (As I remember it, we completely emptied the streetcar.) What a marvelous feeling it was, to stand at the corner and look as Papete pointed out our new home! It happened to be the only house on that side of the street. (The rest was what looked like woods to us.) There were actually only two houses in the whole neighborhood.

The other one was directly across the street, inhabited by a most charming couple (as we found out later) who had come over from France about fifty years earlier.

Just a few seconds after we had left the streetcar, we were standing in our own front yard. The house was small, only three rooms, but of course that mattered little; this was our very own home! The exterior was rough unpainted boards, one-by-twelves, set vertically with battens nailed over the cracks where the boards came together. Inside the walls were wood with a cheesecloth covering to which had been glued some wallpaper.

Conveniences? Well, there weren't any inside bathrooms, no gas, and it would be a number of years before we would have electricity. The only furniture left by the previous tenants was an old wood stove in the kitchen. It was probably too heavy to move out; we felt lucky at not having to bring out another stove. Outside, directly in front of the house, was a drainage ditch about three feet wide and just as deep.

It was spring and, would you believe it, there were plenty of crawfish right in front of the house! It wasn't long before I latched onto a small turtle. Right then I knew I was going to enjoy the neighborhood.

In addition to lots of crawfish, we enjoyed many other dishes using shellfish in our new home. One of my particular favorites was CRAB STEW.

½ cup olive oil or ¼ cup olive oil and ¼ cup vegetable oil
½ cup flour
2 onions, finely chopped
½ bell pepper, finely chopped
1 cup celery, finely chopped
4 cloves garlic, minced
3 oz. tomato paste
1 qt. chicken broth
3 gumbo crabs, cooked and cleaned

2 bay leaves
½ tsp. thyme
½ tsp. basil
¼ tsp. Tabasco
salt and black pepper to taste
1 cup sliced fresh mushrooms
1 lb. crabmeat
6 green onions, finely chopped
cooked rice

First, make a roux with the oil and the flour. Cook the flour in the oil over moderate heat until the flour is brown. Add the onions, bell pepper, celery and garlic; sauté for 3 minutes, stirring frequently. Add the tomato paste and cook for about 5 minutes longer, stirring constantly. Next add the broth, slowly mixing it in, and simmer 5 minutes. Now cut each of the gumbo crabs in half and add to the pot along with the seasonings. Simmer for 20 minutes with the pot partially covered. Now add the mushrooms and the pound of crabmeat and simmer for another 5 minutes. Remove from the heat and add the green onions. Let stand for another 5 minutes before serving over hot, fluffy rice. Serves four to six.

NOTE: These little half-empty crabs are so light they are often called "window-fan crabs" because if you hold them in front of a window fan, they would blow away. They are what we use for gumbo crabs. Because they are so empty, they soak up the seasonings and the flavor of a gumbo or a stew. You can eat them and suck the juice out while eating CRAB STEW.

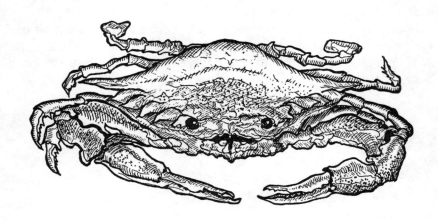

# CRABMEAT-MUSHROOM CASSEROLE

1 lb. crabmeat
2 tbsp. butter plus 3 tbsp.
½ lb. fresh mushrooms,
   sliced
3 tbsp. flour
1½ cups milk
½ tsp. thyme
1 tsp. tarragon leaves

1 tsp. salt
1 tsp. white pepper
⅛ tsp. cayenne pepper
3 dashes Tabasco
⅓ cup dry white wine
1 tsp. Creole mustard
¾ cup seasoned bread
   crumbs

*First, pick all of the shell pieces out of the crabmeat. Then melt the 2 tablespoons of butter in a saucepan. Sauté the mushrooms for 3 or 4 minutes, then set aside.*

*Now over a moderate heat, melt the 3 tablespoons of butter; add the flour and cook over low heat for 3 minutes, stirring constantly. Slowly add the milk and stir until the mixture is well blended and the sauce thickens. Now add the thyme, tarragon, salt, white pepper, cayenne pepper, and Tabasco. Simmer over low heat for 2 or 3 minutes, then add the wine and the mustard. Stir constantly until the sauce is well blended. Add the mushrooms and crabmeat, mix well, and remove from heat.*

*Pour the whole mixture into a well-greased casserole dish and sprinkle with the bread crumbs. Bake for 30 minutes in a preheated 350-degree oven—10 minutes covered, 20 minutes uncovered. Serves four to six.*

# CRAB AND SHRIMP ETOUFFÉE

Onion goggles? What will they think of next? What's going on in the kitchens of America? This train of thought was triggered by a little blurb that I read in the *Times-Picayune*. The article referred to the many difficulties encountered by the average onion chopper and how science and the gadget-makers, after tearful research, had created the perfect solution—onion goggles. *Sacré bleu,* as Memere would have said, this is going too far!

Now, I don't mean to denigrate in the slightest fashion progress in the arts, but I do think the gadgetizing of the American kitchen has been stretched to the breaking point. I'm perfectly willing to tolerate the food processor, even though I believe that hand-chopped onions, celery, bell pepper, and any other vegetables that go into your gumbo, jambalaya, or etouffée have a texture that no electric grinder can ever match. (And, of course, when you're finished chopping by hand, all you do is wash and dry the knife.) And I'll even grudgingly admit that there are a few things that a microwave oven can do faster than the conventional way of cooking, such as melting butter or thawing a package of frozen vegetables or maybe even browning flour for a roux. But, *mes amis,* these machines are taking all of the fun out of cooking! A good case in point would be the preparation of a potful of Creole gumbo. In the microwave it will take maybe three-quarters of an hour, whereas the slow simmering process of Creole cooking consumes three to four hours. In the slower process, however, you have the privilege of playing with the seasoning and bringing the gumbo to the point of perfection. There is also the delight of having your kitchen filled for a few hours with the marvelous aroma of a simmering gumbo. Ah, but chacun à son goût!

But back to the idea of onion goggles. In the first place, I wonder which cooks care to move about in their kitchens looking as though they're ready for the Indianapolis 500. So what do we do about onions? Well, through the years I have run across many so-called remedies, but I must tell you that up to now I have found only one that works. There have been suggestions like holding a kitchen match between your teeth as you chop, or putting a piece of stale bread in your mouth, or slicing off the root end of the onion first, or cutting a cross in the root end of the peeled onion before chopping. But all these procedures will avail you nothing, dear reader. Now let me give you Memere's solution: First, you sharpen your knife to a razor edge. This is so you will cut through the onion, rather than smash it and squeeze out the juice, consequently setting the fumes in motion. (That makes sense, doesn't it?) Secondly, place your onions in the crisper section of your refrigerator. You will find that a cold onion will exude much less vapor than one that is at room temperature. Try it, you'll find it works! And now, since you have a chopped onion on hand, let's use it to construct a CRAB AND SHRIMP ETOUFFEE. Actually, you'll need two medium onions, finely chopped. Here's the recipe.

**3 lbs. raw shrimp**
**1 stick butter**
**4 tbsp. oil**
**2 medium onions, finely**
**chopped**
**½ bell pepper, finely**
**chopped**
**2 ribs celery, finely chopped**
**4 cloves garlic, minced**
**2 cups cold chicken stock**
**1 rounded tbsp. cornstarch**
**¼ cup dry white wine**

**1 tbsp. tomato paste**
**1 bunch finely chopped**
**green onions**
**3 tbsp. minced parsley**
**1 tbsp. Worcestershire**
**sauce**
**salt and black pepper to**
**taste**
**¼ tsp. Tabasco**
**1 lb. crab claw meat**
**cooked rice**

*First peel the shrimp and set them aside. Heat the butter and oil in a cast-iron pot and add the onions, bell pepper, and celery. Sauté for 5 minutes over moderate heat. Add the garlic.*

*To 1 cup of the stock add the cornstarch. Mix well and add this mixture to the pot. Stirring constantly, add the wine, the tomato paste, green onions, parsley, and Worcestershire sauce. Add the shrimp, and simmer for 10 minutes with the pot partially covered, stirring occasionally. During this simmering process the rest of the stock should be added, along with the salt, pepper, and Tabasco. Simmer for 10 minutes, and then add the crabmeat and cook until the meat is thoroughly heated, about 5 minutes. Serve over cooked rice. Serves six to eight.*

# CHEESE AND CRABMEAT CASSEROLE

3 tbsp. butter
4 green onions, minced
½ bell pepper, minced
½ onion, minced
1 rib celery, minced
2 cloves garlic, minced
2 tbsp. flour
1 tomato, peeled, deseeded, and chopped
½ cup dry white wine
⅛ tsp. rosemary
¼ tsp. thyme

1 tsp. salt
¼ tsp. black pepper
¼ tsp. Tabasco
½ tsp. Creole mustard
1 cup heavy cream
1 lb. crab claw meat
⅓ cup shredded cheddar cheese
¼ cup grated mozzarella cheese
2 tbsp. grated Parmesan cheese

*Melt the butter in a skillet and sauté the green onions, bell pepper, onion, and celery over low heat until the vegetables are tender, about 2 minutes, stirring constantly. Add the garlic and cook 2 minutes more. Blend in the flour, then add the tomato and cook for 3 minutes, continuing to stir. Now add the wine, rosemary, thyme, salt, black pepper, Tabasco, and mustard and cook over low heat 5 minutes longer stirring constantly. Still over low heat, add the cream and blend well. Remove the pot from the heat. Gently fold in the crabmeat and the cheddar cheese. Pour the mixture into a well-greased 2-quart casserole dish. Preheat the oven to 350 degrees. Combine the mozzarella and Parmesan cheeses and sprinkle them over the casserole. Bake for 10 to 15 minutes, until the top is browned. Serves four to six.*

# CRAB FRICASSÉE

It would happen two or three times a month, when Memere would get her urge to travel. Of course this was strictly a case of local wanderlust, with the journeys limited to a trip to "town," as Memere was wont to call it. Mamete would laughingly refer to these junkets as "pirooting" around Canal Street! (Don't ask me for the derivation of "piroot"; all I know is that in Mamete's idiom it meant flitting from place to place, which is precisely what Memere did on these excursions.) How did I know what she did? Because I was her sole companion on these trips.

We would leave rather early in the morning to be in town when the stores opened. To get to town we'd walk over to Claiborne and Elysian Fields, which was just a couple of blocks from where we lived, and in about fifteen minutes we would be alighting at Canal and Rampart streets. In and out of the stores we would walk—or sometimes we'd just stop and look in the windows as we proceeded toward the river. One of Memere's favorite places to stop was the Woolworth Five-and-Ten. (In those days it was really a five-and-ten, with no article costing over a dime.) We always referred to the store as Kirby's. I don't know why, except that it must have been Kirby's before it became Woolworth. Memere would usually get me a book from Kirby's, and now it was time for a little lunch. So we'd walk to Royal and down one block to Solari's, one of the remarkable stores in New Orleans at that time. It was always worth a sight-seeing tour around the store, even if you weren't going to buy anything. There were barrels of the most delicious pickles and olives; usually, Memere would buy me a large dill pickle that had an absolutely fabulous taste. (They don't make them like that anymore.) But before we ate our lunch, we'd tour the store and feast with our eyes on the wonderful display of cheeses, the vegetables (which always seemed to be fresher and more colorful than anywhere else), the meats, and, of course, everything else that made this a food emporium unique even in a city as food-conscious as New Orleans.

But finally we would gravitate to the sandwich counter and give our order. It was usually something inexpensive like a hard-boiled egg sandwich. If Memere was really "flush," we might indulge in a remarkably tasty chicken salad on rye. (The rye was Memere's only concession to what she called "health foods.") Having eaten, we would walk down Royal to St. Louis Cathedral, which, by the way, was where Papete had been christened. We'd go in for a few minutes of prayer and then back to Canal Street, where we'd catch the streetcar for the trip home. Sometimes, before we left home in the morning, Mamete would have already started picking the meat from some crabs that had been left over from dinner the night before. And sometimes the crabs wound up in a CRAB FRICASSÉE, which was always a welcome dinnertime treat for two leg-weary travelers.

I have modified this recipe just a bit to make it a little easier to prepare.

**4 large live crabs or 4 large boiled crabs, cleaned and quartered plus 1½ cups crabmeat, preferably claw meat**
**1 qt. water**
**1 tsp. salt**
**2 tbsp. vegetable oil**
**2 tbsp. flour**
**1 onion, minced**
**6 green onions, minced**
**4 cloves garlic, minced**
**1 small bell pepper, finely chopped**
**2 ribs celery, minced**
**2 tbsp. tomato paste**
**1½ lbs. shrimp, peeled and cleaned**
**salt and black pepper to taste**
**¼ tsp. powdered thyme**
**½ tsp. basil**
**3 tbsp. minced fresh parsley**
**2 tbsp. dry sherry**
**cooked rice**

In a 4-quart pot combine the water and salt, bring to a boil and add the crabs. Boil the crabs for about 15 to 20 minutes depending on the size of the crabs. If you buy the crabs already boiled, remove the hard shells and boil the crab shells in salted water, reserving the crab water for stock.

In a cast-iron or heavy-bottomed pot heat the oil and add the flour to make a dark roux. (For detailed instructions on making a dark roux, see index.) Then add the onion, green onions, garlic, bell pepper, and celery and sauté over moderate heat for 5 minutes, stirring constantly. Add the tomato paste and cook 4 or 5 more minutes. Then add the meat from the 4 crabs and 3 cups of the crab water. Partially cover and cook for 20 minutes. Now add the shrimp, the 1½ cups of crabmeat, salt, pepper, thyme, and basil. Simmer for 10 minutes over moderate heat. Now remove from the heat, add the parsley and sherry, and sit down to a bowl of rice and CRAB FRICASSEE—a Creole treat that's hard to beat. Serves four to six.

# SOFT-SHELL CRABS

The soft-shell crab is a delectable dish in New Orleans; it makes a most delicate and savory meal. But you may ask, What is a soft-shell crab? Well, I will tell you.

All crabs periodically outgrow their shells and live for a few hours in a soft-shell state before the new shell begins to harden. The very first time the crab outgrows its shell, the shell splits and the crab creeps out. It is at this point termed a buster crab. All crabs will shed their shells once a month during their first year, less often after that, until they achieve full growth. The trick is to find the crabs at the right moment. Since these soft-shell crabs are harder to come by they are, therefore, more expensive. However, we select the busters as soon as they appear in the seafood market because they are far more tender than the paper shells, which is what they are called after the first shedding. Once we have the busters, we will have a great time planning some special dinners. Just plain fried soft-shell crabs are a great treat. But on occasion, we do them very specially with a meunière or amandine sauce.

# SOFT-SHELL CRABS

8 busters (soft-shell crabs)
1 egg, beaten
3 cups milk
½ tsp. garlic powder
1 tsp. black pepper
½ tsp. cayenne pepper

2 cups flour
1 tsp. salt
3 cups vegetable oil
lemon slices (garnish)
sprigs of fresh parsley
 (garnish)

First, take care to clean the crabs. Wash carefully in cold water, but do not blanch them, because this will destroy their fine, delicate flavor. Remove the spongy feathery substance under the left and right side points. This substance is often called "dead man." Also remove the "sand bag" from beneath the shell just between the eyes by cutting off about ⅓ inch from the front of the head, thus removing the eyes. And be sure to remove the "apron" or "flap." To do this turn the crab over and on the underside there is a semi-circular flap about the size of a quarter. Pull this up and remove. Then wash the crabs well in cold water and dry with a clean towel. Be careful as you handle them because they are quite delicate.

Combine the egg and milk and add the garlic powder, half of the black pepper, and half of the cayenne pepper. Place the crabs in the egg-milk mixture and let them marinate for 10 to 15 minutes.

Combine the flour, salt, and the rest of the black pepper and cayenne pepper in a bowl. Heat the oil to 375 degrees for deep-frying.

Carefully remove the crabs from the milk-egg mixture, let them drain for a few seconds, and then roll them gently in the seasoned flour to coat them thoroughly. Gently shake off excess flour. (Proceed with one crab at a time; if the crabs are small you will be able to fry two at a time.) Fry one or two in the oil for about 8 to 12 minutes, depending on the size. They should be a deep golden brown. Turn them over with tongs while frying to ensure even browning. Lift the crabs out of the oil and drain on paper towels, then remove to a platter and place in a preheated 200-degree oven until all the crabs are fried.

*These are delicious to eat just as they are now. If you wish, garnish with a slice of lemon and a sprig of parsley. Serves four.*

*Note: For a really special dinner make the Meunière Sauce or the Amandine Sauce (see index).*

# CRAWFISH

We have always eaten crawfish and recognized the value of these delicious shellfish. Now their popularity is increasing in the rest of the country. Many local seafood houses are packaging them for deliveries all over the country—from California to Rhode Island and many places in between.

This was another fun-time activity for Leon, our children, and me. With a bucket, a damp burlap sack, and crawfish nets we would go a-crawfishing. After we caught a sackful, we would clean and boil them and gather around our large kitchen table lined with newspaper. As we peeled and ate the crawfish, we would recount the activity of the day. Now and then, we would peel enough crawfish tails to put aside for making a delicious crawfish bisque, or a spicy crawfish etouffée.

If we did not have the time to catch them, we would always buy a sack of crawfish caught in the rice fields. Rice is grown in shallow water, and the crawfish love the slushy, muddy trenches in between the rows of rice, so they breed there prolifically. These crawfish are the cleanest, the tastiest, and the most succulent.

Now, because of the speedy pace of life, we often have to buy the tails fresh in season or frozen from our seafood markets. We enjoy them boiled, in bisque, in etouffée, in pie, in salad, or used to stuff mirlitons.

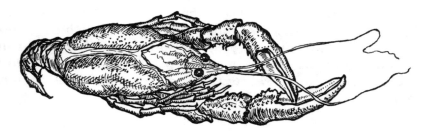

# CRAWFISH PIE

1 pie crust, unbaked with top (see index)
½ stick butter or margarine
½ cup flour
1 cup coarsely chopped onions
⅓ cup coarsely chopped green pepper
⅓ cup coarsely chopped celery
2 cloves garlic, minced

1 tbsp. canned tomato paste
2 bunches green onions, chopped (keep tops separate)
½ tsp. salt
½ tsp. cayenne pepper
½ tsp. black pepper
2 cups water (more may be needed)
3 lbs. crawfish tails
½ cup minced fresh parsley

*Prepare the pastry shell.*

*In a heavy skillet, melt the butter over moderate heat. Add the flour and stirring constantly, make a light brown roux. Add the onions, green pepper, and celery. Cook for about 3 minutes; add the garlic and cook over moderate heat, stirring constantly, until onions are soft. Add the tomato paste, and continue to cook over moderate or low heat, stirring constantly until everything is well mixed. Add the bottom portions of the green onions, the salt, cayenne pepper, black pepper, and the water. Stir well, and simmer partially covered over low heat for about 1 hour. Reduce the liquid by about one-third. The mixture should be creamy and thick. Now add the crawfish tails and simmer for 10 minutes. Then add the green onion tops and the parsley.*

*Pour the crawfish pie filling into the bottom shell. Lightly moisten the outside edge of the crust. Drape the top crust gently over the filling. Cut the top pastry so that it is even with the bottom crust, then crimp the top and bottom crusts together firmly with your fingers or press them together with the tines of a fork. Cut two or three l-inch-long parallel slits about ½ inch apart in the top crust.*

*Bake in the middle of a preheated 350-degree oven for about 45 minutes or until the top crust is golden brown. Serve immediately. Serves six.*

# OYSTERS AND SHRIMP

As you fly in to the Crescent City, you are aware that New Orleans is surrounded by water. Napoleon called us "the Isle of Orleans." We are bound by Lake Pontchartrain on one side and the Mississippi River on the other, and throughout the area there are many bayous, smaller lakes, back bays, inlets, and estuaries.

Because of a particular set of circumstances, we get a bonanza harvest of oysters and shrimp that are considered as unsurpassed by the experts. When the fresh water in the river is low, as it is at the end of the summer and during the fall and winter months, the salty water from the Gulf comes into the Mississippi River. Gradually this water flows into the back bays, inlets, bayous, and estuaries, thus making the water brackish. As the wind shifts and the currents change, the water flows back and forth, and the degree of salinity changes with the motion. At times the water is fresh and then it changes to salty. According to oyster aficionados, the salt water makes oysters salty and the "sweet" (fresh) water makes them fat. This makes our oysters and the shrimp found in these inland waters, which are from 3 feet to 8 feet deep, the greatest found anywhere in the country.

Most of the time we are not concerned with why our shrimp or oysters are good but with how we are going to cook them. One of the ways we enjoy oysters is to have an oyster party. We purchase a sack of oysters and invite family and friends to join us. Equipped with oyster knives and a hearty appetite, the men open the oysters and drink cold beer; meanwhile, the women prepare traditional sauces to accompany the raw oysters. (Ketchup, lemon, horseradish, and a dash of Tabasco make a wonderful sauce.) Some of the oysters are baked on the half-shell with Rockefeller or Bienville sauces. To vary the menu, we may fry some and make oyster "po-boys."

Try the recipe for Oyster Patties—this is a delicious party appetizer, but it is equally appealing as a luncheon or light supper entrée. As a great accompaniment for your turkey dinner or festive holiday meal, try the Oyster Dressing.

Shrimp dishes are another delight. We hold them in the highest esteem! Our menus include such tempting dishes as Shrimp Thermidor and Deep-Fried Shrimp Boulettes. I am sure that many of these recipes will become your favorites just as they are ours.

# BAKED STUFFED OYSTERS

3 doz. large oysters
3 tbsp. butter
2 tbsp. vegetable oil
3 tbsp. flour
2 small onions, minced
1 clove garlic, minced
1 small green pepper,
  minced
1 small rib celery, minced
½ cup coarsely chopped
  fresh mushrooms

2 cups oyster liquor
2 tsp. lemon juice
2 dashes Tabasco
1 tsp. paprika
½ tsp. Worcestershire
  sauce
¼ cup cracker crumbs
salt and pepper to taste
1 tbsp. minced fresh parsley
¼ cup bread crumbs
parsley sprigs (garnish)

*Drain and chop 1 dozen of the oysters into 4 or 5 pieces; set aside. In a heavy saucepan, over moderate heat, melt the butter until just bubbly, then add the oil; when the oil and butter are moderately hot, add the flour. Stir constantly until the flour is a golden-brown color. Now add the onions, garlic, green pepper, and celery, and cook slowly until the onions are transparent. Then add the chopped oysters, mushrooms, oyster liquor, and all of the other ingredients except the bread crumbs. Cook for 10 minutes.*

*Remove the mixture from the heat. Fill the oyster shells with one oyster and a small amount of the sauce. (If you do not have oyster shells, you can use ramekins or any other individual baking dishes.) Make sure you will have enough of the mixture to spoon a teaspoon or two over each of the oysters after baking.*

*Lightly sprinkle with the bread crumbs. Bake in a preheated 350-degree oven for 15 minutes. Place the stuffed shells on serving dishes. Warm the reserved sauce and spoon a little bit over each stuffed oyster. Garnish with parsley sprigs and serve immediately. Serves six.*

*Note: These oysters can be prepared a couple of hours ahead of time, refrigerated, and then baked just before serving.*

# CREOLE OYSTERS

4 doz. oysters and their
  liquor
½ stick butter
2 carrots, chopped
1 cup chopped onions
1 cup finely chopped celery
2 tbsp. chopped parsley
1 tsp. paprika

½ tsp. powdered thyme
½ tsp. marjoram
2 bay leaves
1 tsp. salt
1 cup light cream
2 tbsp. tomato paste
2 tbsp. flour
2 tbsp. water

*Try to get freshly shucked oysters. Drain them and reserve the liquor. Melt the butter in a large saucepan and add the carrots, onions, and celery. Sauté until the vegetables are tender, about 5 minutes. Add the oyster liquor and cook until it has almost evaporated. Then add the parsley, paprika, thyme, marjoram, bay leaves, and salt, and simmer for 10 minutes. Next add the oysters and simmer until their edges curl (about 5 minutes). Add the cream and tomato paste. Mix the flour with the water and stir into the oyster mixture. Simmer for about 5 minutes, stirring constantly until the sauce has thickened. Serves six to eight.*

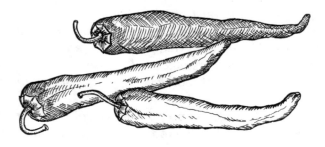

# OYSTERS FLORENTINE

There is an old saying to the effect that there is nothing so permanent as change. I thought about that as I was trying to pinpoint some of the forces that have brought about so many changes in the decades since I was a boy and on up to the present time. As I thought further, it became very clear to me that the two most potent forces affecting our daily lives are the automobile and the air conditioner. I don't think that most of us even begin to realize how the motorcar has changed our daily routine. Do you realize how reclusive our society has become? If, for example, we need something from a store six blocks away, it's into the car and on to the store. On the way there we meet no one; we are alone with our thoughts, and, unless we are involved in a little fender-bumping, we remain in "solitary."

Let me contrast this routine with life a few years ago and the way Memere would get to the French Market and other stores in our neighborhood. As she walked out of the house, there most certainly would be housewives, either going to the stores, scrubbing the front steps, cleaning the sidewalk, or just exchanging a little gossip. Before she got to the corner, four or five neighbors had already been greeted and pleasantries exchanged. This process would continue all the way to the store and back. There was never a time when Memere didn't know who was sick, having a baby, graduating from school, on the "outs" with her husband, or having financial problems. Now this knowledge did not stem from just plain curiosity, but rather a deep feeling of concern; you had to have feelings about people you came in contact with almost every day. Somehow our automobiles have almost eliminated that intimate association with our neighbors.

There are many other changes we could attribute to the auto, but let's move on to the air conditioner. That's the infernal machine that literally drove people inside. Yes, before the air began to get cooled inside, there was only one place where a little relief from the heat could be had, and that was *outside*. When the mercury rose, all of the families on the block would be sitting outside, palmetto fans waving in hand, creating a little breeze. It was then that neighbor would greet neighbor and the latest news would be discussed and issues argued.

But with the birth of the air conditioner, fraternization with the neighbors has gone the way of the dodo bird. At this point in my ruminations a rather devilish thought came to mind. Maybe all isn't lost. Maybe we are near a point where energy will become scarce enough so that the use of air conditioning will be banned and—for a further improvement—gasoline will become almost unobtainable! Oh, you dreamer, you!

As we sit and reminisce about the old neighborhood, we remember that out of our past history comes many great oyster recipes. Then, as now, we have delicious oysters and on a cool, brisk autumn day our internal time clock reminds us that it's time for an oyster dinner. Here's a recipe that was always a favorite—OYSTERS FLORENTINE.

**6 tbsp. butter plus 2 tbsp.**
**6 tbsp. flour**
**2 cups chicken broth**
**2 cups cream**
**4 egg yolks**
**½ cup grated Swiss Cheese**
**2 tbsp. grated Parmesan cheese**
**salt and black pepper to taste**
**2 tbsp. lemon juice**
**2 to 3 doz. fresh oysters with their liquor**
**2 10-oz. pkgs. frozen spinach**
**¼ tsp. Tabasco**
**paprika (garnish)**

*First, melt the 6 tablespoons butter in a skillet. Add the flour, and cook over low heat for 5 minutes, stirring constantly. Slowly stir in the chicken broth. Now, beat together the cream and egg yolks and add to the skillet. Mix well, and then add the Swiss and Parmesan cheeses and cook over very low heat for 5 more minutes, stirring constantly. Season with salt, pepper, and lemon juice. Cover and set over a double boiler to keep warm.*

*In a saucepan place the oysters and the oyster liquor and over moderate heat simmer for about 4 or 5 minutes only, until the oyster edges curl. Drain oysters. Reserve the liquor. Boil the spinach using the oyster liquor according to directions and drain, then beat 2 tablespoons butter into the spinach pot and add the Tabasco.*

Spread half the spinach over the bottom of a casserole dish and then lay the poached oysters and half the sauce over it. Now top this with the remainder of the spinach. Pour the remaining cheese sauce over the top. Place the casserole under the broiler until lightly browned. At this point remove from the oven, sprinkle with a little paprika and serve. Serves four to six.

## OYSTER PATTIES

3 doz. shucked raw oysters
  with their liquor
4 tbsp. butter plus 3 tbsp.
2 bunches green onions,
  minced
½ cup minced celery
2 cloves garlic, minced
4 tbsp. all-purpose flour
1 cup oyster liquor

2 tbsp. light cream
black pepper and Tabasco
  to taste
salt (may not be necessary if
  the oysters are salty)
juice of ½ lemon
¼ cup minced parsley
3 doz. cocktail pastry shells

In a saucepan, poach the oysters in their own liquor for 5 minutes, then drain, reserving the liquor. Check the oysters for grit or shells; then chop the oysters finely.

Melt the 4 tablespoons of butter in a heavy saucepan over moderate heat. Sauté the green onions, celery, and garlic until the celery is soft. Add the flour to make a blond roux and stir constantly over low heat. Simmer for 5 minutes, then stir the oyster liquor into the roux, stirring constantly. Simmer for 5 minutes; now slowly add the cream, stirring constantly. Simmer for 3 to 5 minutes and then add the pepper, Tabasco, and oysters. Simmer over low heat for 5 minutes and then taste the sauce to adjust seasonings, adding salt if needed. Add the 3 tablespoons of butter, the lemon juice, and the parsley. Mix well. Fill the pastry shells and bake in a preheated 370-degree oven for 5 to 7 minutes. Yield: enough to fill 3 dozen small pastry shells or 12 large pastry shells.

# OYSTER DRESSING

Oyster dressing is one of our favorites for a festive turkey. Here is an old Creole specialty, a favorite with the Soniat family. This is another version for you to try in place of the ever-popular cornbread dressing.

**4 doz. small oysters and their liquor (2 cups, if possible)**
**4 cups cubed stale French bread**
**2 lbs. lean ground meat**
**1 large onion, finely chopped**
**½ cup finely chopped celery**
**2 cloves garlic, minced**
**1 tsp. salt (if oysters are salty, you may need less)**
**1 tsp. black pepper**
**1 tsp. poultry seasoning**
**1 tsp. thyme**
**1 bay leaf**
**½ tsp. cayenne pepper**
**3 dashes Tabasco**
**1 cup chicken stock**
**2 eggs, slightly beaten**
**1 bunch green onions, coarsely chopped**
**½ cup minced fresh parsley**
**¼ cup bread crumbs (needed if excess liquid is present)**

*Use freshly shucked oysters; check for any shells. Poach the oysters by placing them and their liquor in a large, heavy skillet. Simmer over low heat. When the edges of the oysters curl (about 5 minutes), remove them and coarsely chop. Add all of the oyster liquor to the bread cubes; mash the bread in the liquid and break it into little pieces, then set it aside.*

*Place the ground meat in a heavy cast-iron pot; add the onion, celery, and garlic; cook over moderate heat, stirring frequently. When the meat has lost any red or pink color and the onions and celery are soft, add the bread soaked in the oyster liquor. Stir well. Now add the salt, black pepper, poultry seasoning, thyme, bay leaf, cayenne pepper, Tabasco, and chicken stock. Mix very well; cook over low to moderate heat for 1 hour.*

*Add the oysters and cook for 30 minutes more, stirring frequently. Remove from the heat, add the beaten eggs, green onions, and parsley, and mix well. If excess liquid is present (more* than ¼ cup), add ¼ cup bread crumbs (or a bit more, if needed). Stir until everything is well mixed, then let the stuffing cool.

If you make the dressing a day ahead of time, it will enhance the flavor. However, be sure to refrigerate it overnight once it has cooled. This will stuff a 15- to 18-pound turkey.

A note of caution: A turkey or chicken should never be stuffed until just before it is going to be cooked, because the stuffing mixture may sour inside and spoil the meat.

For detailed instructions on the baking of a turkey, see La Bouche Creole.

# OYSTER PO-BOY

There is no better place in the world to eat fried oysters than here in New Orleans, and no better way to have them than in a crisp, hot loaf of French bread with a few shreds of lettuce and some thinly sliced tomatoes, a pickle, and a wedge of lemon. The oysters are dipped in flour, then in an egg-milk mixture, then in cornmeal, and fried quickly in deep fat. Like the bread, they are crisp, hot, and incredibly good.

In New Orleans the oyster loaf is known as the "médiatrice." According to tradition, when a nineteenth-century New Orleans husband had spent the night in the French Quarter either drinking or gambling at cards, an oyster loaf was brought home to his wife as a "médiatrice" or peacemaker. When the aroma of this delicious sandwich assailed her nostrils, we are told, all was forgiven. The sandwich is also called a "poor boy" (pronounced "po-boy") by local residents. "Poor boys" are also popular made with roast beef, ham and cheese, and hot sausage. Here's how to make an OYSTER PO-BOY.

**2 doz. oysters, freshly shucked if possible**
**¼ tsp. cayenne pepper**
**¼ tsp. black pepper**
**1 egg**
**¼ cup milk**
**½ tsp. salt (may need less if oysters are salty)**
**1 cup flour**
**1 cup yellow cornmeal**

**1 cup vegetable oil**
**1 loaf warm French bread (about 18 inches long)**
**8 tbsp. melted butter**
**1 cup finely shredded lettuce**
**1 large tomato, thinly sliced**
**dill pickle, sliced**
**lemon wedge (garnish)**

*Drain oysters, discarding any shell bits, and pat them dry with paper toweling. Sprinkle lightly with cayenne and black pepper. In a shallow bowl beat the egg until frothy. Add the milk and salt and mix well. Dip the oysters first in the flour, then the egg-milk mixture, and finally the cornmeal. Deep-fry in vegetable oil at 360 degrees. Don't crowd the pot—put only six at a time and fry until the coating is crisp* and golden brown. This should not take more than 2 to 3 minutes. Transfer the fried oysters to paper towels to drain.

To assemble the po-boy, brush warm French bread with melted butter, add the fried oysters, the shredded lettuce, and slices of tomato and dill pickle. Cut the loaf in half. Serve with lemon wedge. Serves two.

# SHRIMP YVETTE

1 stick butter
2 lbs. shrimp (26 to 35 to the
  count), peeled and
  deveined
1 cup finely chopped green
  onions

¼ cup white wine or sherry
4 slices toast or 4 pastry
  shells
Béchamel sauce (recipe
  follows)

Melt the butter in a saucepan and sauté the shrimp and the green onions. When the onions are limp, add the wine. Cook until the shrimp turn pink, about 10 minutes. Add them to the béchamel sauce before serving.

To prepare the béchamel sauce:

1 stick butter
½ cup flour
1 cup shrimp stock
1 cup light cream

4 drops Tabasco
¼ tsp. freshly ground
  nutmeg
½ tsp. salt

Melt the butter in a heavy saucepan over moderate heat. Add the flour, stirring constantly. Do not brown. When the flour is thoroughly blended, gradually add the stock and the cream. Allow to cook slowly until it is well blended and has begun to thicken, about 5 minutes. Then add the Tabasco, nutmeg, and salt.

Add the prepared shrimp to the sauce. Stir gently. When the shrimp are thoroughly warm, about 5 minutes, serve over toast or pastry shells. Serves four.

# DEEP-FRIED SHRIMP BOULETTES

2 lbs. raw shrimp (31–35 to
  the count)
1 tbsp. butter
⅓ cup finely chopped bell
  pepper
⅓ cup finely chopped celery
3 tbsp. finely chopped onion
6 green onions, finely
  chopped
1 large egg, lightly beaten
¾ tsp. salt
¾ tsp. black pepper
¼ tsp. cayenne pepper
dash Tabasco
2 cups stale bread, cut in
  1-inch cubes

2 tbsp. milk
3 tbsp. finely chopped fresh
  parsley
¾ cup finely chopped water
  chestnuts
2 tsp. lemon juice
1 cup flour
1 tsp. black pepper
¼ tsp. cayenne pepper
½ tsp. salt
½ tsp. paprika
1 egg
¼ cup milk
1 cup Italian bread crumbs
1½ cups vegetable oil

Peel the shrimp and steam them until they are pink and tender, then chop them very finely.

Melt the butter in a skillet and, over moderate heat, sauté the bell pepper, celery, onion, and green onions for 3 or 4 minutes, just until the vegetables begin to get soft. (You want some texture.) Remove from the heat and set aside to cool.

Lightly beat the egg and season with the salt, ¾ teaspoon black pepper, ¼ teaspoon cayenne pepper, and Tabasco.

In a large mixing bowl, place the shrimp, bread, milk, parsley, and water chestnuts; mix well. Add the egg mixture and blend everything together. Now add the sautéed vegetables and the lemon juice to the bowl. Chill the mixture for 1 hour, then mix with your hands. Shape the mixture into little balls (boulettes in French) about 1 inch in diameter. Chill in the refrigerator for 30 minutes.

Roll the boulettes in the flour mixed with the 1 teaspoon black pepper, ¼ teaspoon cayenne pepper, salt, and paprika; shake off any excess. Now mix the egg and the milk together (this is called an *egg wash). Dip the boulettes in the "egg wash" and roll in the bread crumbs. Deep-fry the boulettes in oil at 375 degrees until they are golden brown. (Don't overcrowd the fry pan.) Serve with the Tangy Spicy Sauces (recipes follow). Yield: 25 to 30 boulettes.*

# TANGY SPICY SAUCES

*Sauce #1*

**4 tbsp. apricot preserves**
**2 tbsp. vinegar**
**2 tbsp. sugar**
**2 tbsp. water**

*Combine the above and stir well.*

*Sauce #2*

**Equal proportions of:**
**Hot jalapeño relish**
**apricot preserves**

*Combine the above and stir well.*

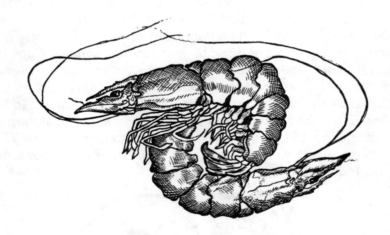

# MARINATED SHRIMP
## WITH
## MUSHROOMS AND OLIVES

2 lbs. raw shrimp (26 to 30
   the count)
½ cup olive oil
juice of 1 lemon
2 cloves garlic, minced
1¼ tsp. salt
½ tsp. black pepper
¼ tsp. cayenne pepper
½ tsp. thyme
⅛ tsp. nutmeg

2 bay leaves
2 white onions, thinly sliced
1½ cups sliced fresh
   mushrooms
4 green onions, minced
1 tbsp. minced parsley
½ cup pimentos, chopped
½ cup whole, small, stuffed
   olives

*Place the raw shrimp in a pot of boiling water. When the water returns to a boil, cook for 3 or 4 minutes until the shrimp are pink. Drain and plunge the shrimp into ice-cold water for 10 minutes. Remove the heads and peel the shrimp. Set aside.*

*Combine the next 10 ingredients (beginning with the olive oil) in a saucepan; bring to a boil and then reduce to a simmer. Cook for 5 minutes or until the onions are transparent. Remove from the heat, add the mushrooms and the green onions and mix well.*

*Combine the rest of the ingredients in a large bowl. Add the shrimp. Pour the mixture from the saucepan over the shrimp and toss lightly to mix. Cover and refrigerate for at least 6 hours. This is delicious served over salad greens as a luncheon or supper entrée. Serves four to six.*

# HOW TO BOIL SHELLFISH

3 gallons water
2 lemons, sliced
3 large unpeeled onions,
  sliced
3 ribs celery, with leaves,
  cut in large pieces
1 hot chili pepper or ½ tsp.
  cayenne pepper
4 whole pods of garlic

4 bay leaves
1 cup seafood boiling
  seasoning (recipe follows,
  or you can use
  commercial crab boil)
½ cup salt
20 lbs. live crawfish or 3
  dozen live crabs or 15 lbs.
  large raw shrimp

Combine all the ingredients except for the seafood in a large enamelware pot, and bring to a boil over high heat. Cover tightly, reduce the heat to low, and simmer for at least 20 minutes. This simmering liquid is called a courtbouillon. (A courtbouillon is any seasoned liquid in which seafood is boiled or poached.)

While the courtbouillon simmers, clean the shellfish. Wash the shrimp and crawfish thoroughly with lots of cold, running water. If you are boiling crawfish, you must purge them as follows: soak the live crawfish in cold salted water for 15 minutes. Do this several times. Be sure to throw away any dead crawfish. When the seafood has been washed, it is ready to cook.

Increase the heat under the courtbouillon and when the water is at a rolling boil, add the seafood. The water will stop boiling with the addition of the seafood, so cover the pot. When the water comes back to a boil, start timing: 3 to 5 minutes for shrimp; 3 to 4 minutes for crawfish; and 10 to 12 minutes for crabs.

You don't want to overcook these delicacies! To enhance the flavor turn off the heat, and add one quart of ice-cold water to stop the cooking process. Then remove the pot from the heat and allow the seafood to soak in the liquid for 30 minutes to absorb more of the flavoring.

Note: We add small new Irish potatoes and corn on the cob to the courtbouillon 10 or 15 minutes before we add the seafood. This makes a full and appetizing meal.

# SEAFOOD BOILING SEASONING

¼ cup mustard seeds
¼ cup coriander seeds
1 tbsp. marjoram
2 tbsp. dill seeds
1 tbsp. thyme
2 tbsp. whole allspice

1 tbsp. ground cloves
1 tbsp. celery seeds
4 chili peppers or 1 tsp.
cayenne pepper
4 bay leaves, crumbled

*Mix all the ingredients very well and place in a jar. Cover tightly and store at room temperature. Will keep 3 or 4 months. Yield: 1 cup.*

# SHRIMP THERMIDOR

2 cups Anita's Mornay
Sauce (see index)
4 lbs. shrimp, peeled and
deveined
6 tbsp. butter
¼ cup finely chopped white
onion
½ cup finely chopped green
onions

½ cup dry white wine
2 tbsp. Creole mustard
1 tbsp. minced fresh parsley
2 tbsp. whipping cream
3 tbsp. freshly grated
Parmesan cheese

*Prepare the Mornay Sauce and set aside. Melt 4 tablespoons of the butter in a saucepan and sauté the shrimp until they turn pink and tender, about 5 minutes. Remove the shrimp and set aside. In the same pan add 2 tablespoons of butter and sauté the onion and green onions over low to moderate heat stirring constantly. Add the wine and cook 3 minutes more. Add the mustard, parsley, and Mornay Sauce and stir until well blended. Slice the shrimp in half lengthwise and add the shrimp and whipping cream to the saucepan, blending everything together. Pour into a buttered casserole dish. Sprinkle with the grated Parmesan cheese and brown lightly under a broiler for about 2 minutes. Serves six to eight.*
*This is delicious either in pastry shells or over toast or boiled rice.*

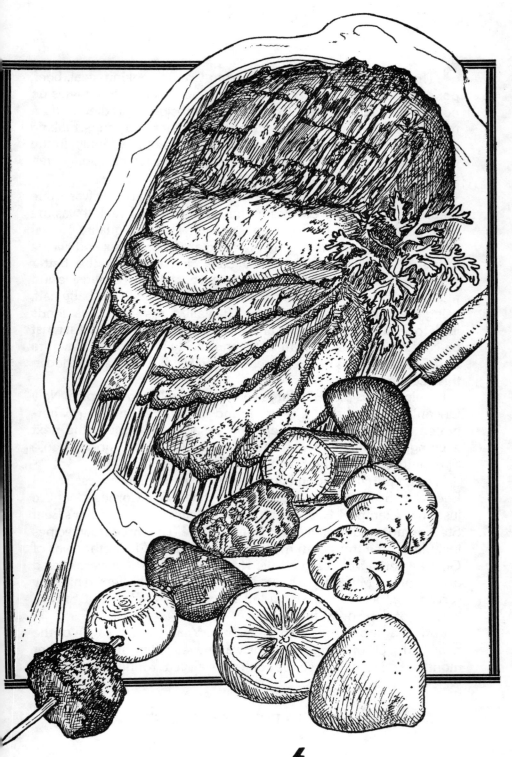

*meats*

There is a variety of meats used in Creole cooking: veal, beef, pork, and an assortment of wild game. However, Creole meals do not always feature a meat dish as the principal ingredient. Often meat is used to flavor the favorite one-pot dishes and soups, making a modest amount of meat go a long way in feeding a family. In the use of meats, as in other areas of cooking, the Creoles display their talent for being economical as well as creative.

Veal was always a favorite with Europeans and so it was quite natural that the early Creoles preferred the taste of veal. It was the most popular meat for everyday cooking. The best quality of veal comes from calves that are milk-fed and are between six and twelve weeks old. The meat is a very pale pink color. In the better restaurants, this kind of veal is still served, but it is very expensive and rather scarce. So the Creole home cook must settle for baby calf, using the palest meat she can find (usually a rosy red). Veal lends itself to a variety of flavorings and sauces. Because it lacks fat, it must be cooked carefully. (It can toughen quickly.) One of our favorite ways to serve veal is Panéed (breaded and fried), a recipe included in this section.

Ethnic groups played a large role in the evolution of typical New Orleanian meat dishes. Creoles found themselves enjoying Sauerbraten one evening and preparing Lasagne Bolognese the next evening; you will find recipes for these and also for a good Creole Spaghetti Sauce in the following pages.

We can purchase good beef, and we use it in many ways: Boiled Beef with Scallion Sauce, Stuffed Meatloaf, and Corned Beef are just a few examples. Beef can be prepared simply as in Mother's Beef Stew or more elaborately as in Daube Glacé. The three stew recipes included come from both my family and Leon's. My mother was of German heritage; her stews called for cubed potatoes or were served over noodles. My father, a south Louisiana native, preferred his stew served over rice. I've also included a recipe for Papete's Veal Stew, a favorite of the Soniat family.

Pork is a popular meat in the winter. Years ago, because of the heat and lack of refrigeration, it was never eaten in the summer months. Today, of course, we cook pork all year round. We use ham or pickle pork for seasonings. We also have wonderful sausages that we use in our gumbos and jambalayas. You may want to try making your very own Chaurice Sausage.

Wild game, which the Creoles used because it was so plentiful, is not easy to come by today. But at one time, New Orleans cooks were famous for their wild game dishes. Venison is not sold in markets today, but every now and then a hunting friend shares his bounty and gives me a leg of venison, which I like to roast. I've included my recipe for this savory dish; I hope you enjoy it as well as the other recipes in this section.

# BOILED BEEF WITH SCALLION SAUCE

About one out of three communications I receive from readers contains questions about cast-iron cookware, and so I want to devote some space to the cast-iron pot, the greatest cooking invention since the wok. Why such praise? Let's consider cost first. The price you'll pay for a good cast-iron pot is about one-third what you'd shell out for an enamelware or stainless-steel cook pot, and about half that for a good, heavy aluminum utensil. So save your money. Durability? They'll last forever! I use pots today that Memere cooked with, and there are still, I would estimate, a couple of centuries more left in them. Actually, the longer they're used the better they function. Can you damage them? Yes, if you drop them into a smelter or bang them with an eight-pound maul, but banging on their sides with metal spoons does no damage whatsoever, unlike the effect on their enamel or aluminum counterparts.

So, in buying our cast-iron pots, what do we look for? At the risk of seeming chauvinistic, I recommend none but pots cast here in America. Lately there has been a surge of activity in the cast-iron pot field, and so we've experienced a plethora of importations. Eschew these pots like the plague; buy those made in this country, and you'll be getting a superior pot. The foreign product lacks the density and solidity of our domestic pots and is much harder to season.

Where are they found? Almost any store handling cookware will have a few cast-iron pots in stock. You will find some with smooth, others with rough interiors; get the smooth interiors, if possible. They are easier to season and keep clean.

So we've made our purchase and now it's time to season the pot. First, get a soapy steel-wool pad and spend about half an hour scouring the inside of the pot, bottom, and sides. Rinse with warm water and place the pot on the stove, over very low heat. (This is to dry the pot thoroughly.) While the pot is drying, do the same to the inside of the cover. It is astounding how rarely any attention is given to the covers; this neglect results in periodic rusting. Now, back to the pot, which, by now, should be thoroughly dry. Remove it from the heat and place the cover on the burner to dry. Our next step is to oil or grease the inside of the pot. Sometimes we use ham fat for this, rubbing the warm pot inside with the fat until it is thoroughly coated. If you have no ham fat available, use cooking oil. When the inside is greased or oiled, place it on the burner and heat it slowly for 5 minutes, then remove it and allow it to cool to the point where it can be handled. Rub the inside briskly with paper toweling. Repeat the process three or four times, or until the paper towel remains clean after you use it to wipe the inside. At this point spread a thin coating of oil inside, and your pot will be seasoned. (Don't forget the cover; do likewise.)

Now to put it to use. A seasoned pot has to be used at least once a week. If the pot sits on a shelf, unused, for a considerable period of time, the oil or grease will become rancid (of course, if it's not seasoned, the pot will rust). To wash the pot after using it, use plain, warm water (no soap or detergent), dry it well, and occasionally coat the interior with a little oil before putting it away. Well, now that it's seasoned, how about trying it out with BOILED BEEF WITH SCALLION SAUCE?

4 lbs. boneless beef chuck or lean brisket
water (enough to cover the meat by 2 inches)
2 carrots, scraped and sliced
3 ribs celery, cut in 3-inch pieces
1 large onion, quartered
5 sprigs fresh parsley
½ tsp. freshly ground black pepper
2 tsp. salt
½ stick butter
3 tbsp. flour
½ cup light cream
1 bunch green onions, finely chopped
½ tsp. freshly ground nutmeg

*Place the meat in a cast-iron pot and pour in enough water to cover the meat by 2 inches. Bring to a boil and then reduce to a simmer. Let it cook for 30 minutes; meanwhile, skim off the scum that rises to the surface. When no more scum is apparent, add the carrots, celery, onion, parsley, pepper, and salt and simmer for 2½ to 3 hours, partially covered, until the meat is tender. Transfer the meat to a platter and keep it warm. Strain the liquid into a bowl and set it aside. Put the vegetables in a stock pot or discard.*

*Melt the butter in the cast-iron pot. Add the flour and cook over low heat, stirring constantly, for about 3 minutes. Slowly pour in 2 cups of the strained liquid and then the cream. Raise the heat. Stir the sauce until it is almost boiling; reduce the heat and simmer for about 5 minutes. Add the green onions and nutmeg, stir, and the sauce is ready.*

*To serve, slice the meat rather thickly and spoon some of the sauce over the meat. Place the remaining sauce in a warm serving bowl to be used as needed. This is a wonderful way to christen your newly seasoned pot. Serves eight to ten.*

# CORNED BEEF

A short time ago I thought about, and immediately developed a yen for, some good old-fashioned, homemade corned beef, and so I set about preparing some. I remembered how Memere would pickle her beef. The most wonderful aroma floated across the kitchen while the corned beef was marinating. Let me tell you what you could really enjoy about Memere's kitchen. First, there was always something going on. There were always a few cream cheeses in their little metal molds on the drainboard and the faint smell of the curdled milk as it drained. Wine and beer were always fermenting in the crocks that stood against the wall, adding their delicious aromas to the rest. I pause to remind you that since air conditioning hadn't even been heard of, no fans were moving these delightful smells away from the kitchen. But let's go on. Against the wall were little brown paper bags. The bags were closed tightly and bound with string, and there were little branches sticking out of the bags. This was the way Memere would dry her seasonings. Memere grew her own herbs, and, of course, used them fresh whenever it could be done. The surplus was put in a paper bag. This very ingenious way of preparing dried seasonings worked like this: As the seasonings dried, the bags were shaken and the leaves or flowers or berries would come loose from the stems and fall into the bags. When the branches were bare they were removed; now the bags contained the important part of the plant. Can you imagine what a delightful blend the seasonings would add to the kitchen smell?

But I began this exposition by developing a yen for some good corned beef, and so I fixed some just as Memere had taught me. From my friendly butcher I got a nice piece of top roast (about 5 pounds). I cut the roast into pieces no more than 3 inches thick. (This is done so that the brine will have a better chance to penetrate through the meat.) Next I laid the meat in an enameled pot; do not use aluminum or cast-iron pots. Then I covered the meat with water, added about 3 extra inches, and then poured the water out into another pot. This was done to determine the right amount of water to use. I then took a raw egg (in the shell) and placed it in the water and began to add salt. How much salt? The way Memere did it, she would add salt, stir it to dissolve, and keep adding salt until the egg began to float. This indicated that the water was salty enough. Now remove the egg; next, the water was heated, and 2 chopped onions, 4 cloves of mashed garlic, a dozen whole peppercorns, ½ teaspoon thyme, and ½ teaspoon Tabasco were added. After it had boiled or 5 minutes uncovered, the water was poured over the meat. You must not forget that the meat has to be weighted down. Otherwise it will float! So a large soup plate was placed on top of the meat, and the pot was covered. It takes 10 to 12 days for the meat to become pickled. During that time it can be stirred three or four times.

At this point, I digress for a moment to explain that in most recipes for corned beef, one of the ingredients found is saltpeter. Memere never used saltpeter and made a point of explaining that it was unnecessary. It served only to make the meat come out a red color, but more than that, it was another chemical the human system could do without, so when you decide to make your own corned beef, forget the saltpeter.

Now I placed the pot in the refrigerator. After 10 or 12 days the beef was ready. I removed it from the brine and soaked the meat for 2 hours in cool fresh water to remove the salty flavor.

Now I drained the meat and placed it in stock pot, covered it with fresh water. I put 1 can (1.25 ounces) of whole mixed pickling spice in a double layer of cheesecloth, knotted the cloth, and then placed it in the pot. I let it come to a boil first, then reduced the heat and simmered it until it was tender; this took an hour or so. When the beef was tender, I removed it from the pot and cut it into thin slices. To really top it off, add 2 heads (or 3 lbs.) of cabbage, plus a few small Irish potatoes, to the broth in the stock pot and simmer for an additional 30 minutes. Serve with hot French bread so that you can fully enjoy every drop of the "potlikker." Serves eight.

5 lbs. top beef round roast
water (enough to cover the
    meat by 3 inches)
1 uncooked egg (in shell)
salt (see procedure)
2 onions, chopped
4 cloves garlic, mashed
1 doz. whole peppercorns

½ tsp. thyme
½ tsp. Tabasco
water (to cover the roast)
1 1.25-oz. can whole mixed
    pickling spice
3 lbs. cabbage, quartered
8 to 10 small Irish potatoes

# MOTHER'S BEEF STEW

4 tbsp. vegetable oil
1½ lbs. boneless stew beef
1 lb. stew beef (with bone)
4 tbsp. flour
2 large onions, coarsely
  chopped
1 large bell pepper, coarsely
  chopped
3 ribs celery, coarsely
  chopped
3 cloves garlic, minced
4 oz. tomato puree
3 cups water or beef stock

2 bay leaves
½ tsp. thyme
½ tsp. allspice
1 tsp. salt
½ tsp. black pepper
dash Tabasco
2 carrots, cut in quarters
3 medium potatoes, peeled
  and cut in ¾-inch cubes
¼ cup finely chopped green
  onions
3 tbsp. minced fresh parsley

Heat the oil in a Dutch oven and brown the meat, turning until all pieces are browned nicely. Remove to a platter. Add the flour and make a rich dark brown roux over moderate heat, stirring constantly. When the roux is ready, add the onions, bell pepper, and celery. Cook over moderate heat, stirring constantly, for about 3 or 4 minutes, then add the garlic and simmer until the onions are soft. Add the tomato puree and simmer for 3 or 4 minutes, stirring constantly. Add the beef stock or water, the bay leaves, thyme, allspice, salt, black pepper, and Tabasco and stir until it is well mixed. Now return the meat to the pot. Bring to a simmer and cook, partially covered, for 2 hours. Add the carrots and potatoes and cook for 30 minutes. Check to see if the meat is tender. (When pierced easily with a fork, the meat is done.) Check from time to time to see if more water is needed. Taste to adjust seasonings.

When ready to serve, add the green onions and the parsley. Serves four to six

NOTE: If you wish to vary this recipe, skip the potatoes and serve over buttered noodles. A green salad is all you need for a complete meal and, of course, French bread to enjoy every drop of the gravy.

# DAUBE GLACÉ

Recently, struck with a bit of nostalgia, I began to "set my mouth," as Mamete would say, for some good, old-fashioned daube glacé. Now I stress "old-fashioned" to differentiate it from the gelatin-loaded glacé that is usually served as today's version of one of the tastiest of the Creole classic dishes. With my usual single-mindedness, I then decided that the only way I could enjoy the treat was to cook up a dish of it myself. There were many times when I would accompany Memere to the French Market for the necessary ingredients: the cut of meat (usually it was a piece of lean shoulder) and the bag of bones necessary for the gel. I knew the process well, having participated so many times, and so I roused myself and journeyed over to see my favorite butcher at Sclafani's Meat Market, a place where I can still get meat cut to my own specifications. I bought a nice six-pound piece of lean shoulder and about ten pounds of bones. I selected some bones from the back legs, but most from the front legs of the cow, because that's where most of the jelly would come from (gel from the front legs and marrow richness from the hind legs). Back home, the first thing was to set the bones to soaking. Off the shelf came the stock pot. The bones were rinsed and packed tightly into the pot, and then water was added to cover the bones (enough water so that there was an inch or so to spare over the bones). Now the heat was turned on, very low, and the pot was set to simmer. It's important in making stock that the water comes very slowly to a simmer. This will keep the liquid from becoming cloudy and the stock will not have to be clarified. As the stock simmered, a scum began to rise to the surface; this was skimmed off. This went on for about an hour and a half and then, when the pot quit "scumming," the seasoning was added. This consisted of 3 onions, each sliced in half and added, unpeeled, to the stock (the brown of the peeling will color the stock); a pod of garlic (this is a *whole* garlic); a few ribs of celery; 3 or 4 peeled and sliced carrots; 5 or 6 bay leaves, and about a tablespoon of whole peppercorns. You can also throw in a sliced lemon. (At this stage, no ground seasoning was added; if you wish to add thyme, add the leaves, but any ground seasoning will only cloud the stock.) And so the stock simmered, without any stirring, for 4 hours.

Now while the stock was cooking, our attention was given to the meat. The meat had to be cooked, but first is was browned. The browning kept the juices in the meat while it was being braised. The easiest way to do this was in the broiler. I placed the meat on a rack and broiled each side to a deep, delicious-looking brown (about 12 to 15 minutes). When this was accomplished, the meat was then placed in a deep pot for braising. To this pot with the meat I added 2 sliced onions and a chopped bell pepper. I removed enough liquid from the stock pot to come up almost to the top of the meat and then set the whole thing to simmering. I then had two pots simmering—the stock pot and the meat pot. About every 15 minutes, I turned the meat in the pot, but never, at any time, stirred or disturbed the bones in the stock pot in any way; to do so would have clouded the stock! The cooking continued until the meat was tender, about 3 to 3½ hours. (The meat is cooked if it is tender when pierced with a fork or skewer.) The meat was removed from the pot and allowed to cool. The liquid was strained and set aside.

The stock pot was removed from the heat. When the pot cooled the bones were removed and the stock was strained.

I then combined the stock and the reserved meat juices, adding the salt, pepper, allspice, cayenne pepper, and Tabasco. (Dispense these seasonings with a heavy hand; you must overseason this liquid because as it gels the seasoning seems to disappear.)

I cut the meat into lengths of approximately 2 inches by 3 inches and ¼ inch thick. Then I assembled the daube glacé. First, I put 2 or 3 slices of the lemon and a couple of sprigs of parsley on the bottom of two rectangular 3-quart molds. (This will eventually be the decorated top of the glacé.) I gently poured about ½ cup of the seasoned liquid into the molds and set it in the refrigerator to harden. This took about half an hour. I removed it from the refrigerator and poured in a little more of the liquid to seal in the lemon and parsley and allowed it to harden again. Then I very carefully laid the meat in the molds and slowly ladled enough liquid so that it barely covered the meat and once again placed the molds in the refrigerator. When this had jelled I added enough liquid to come to about ½ inch above the meat level and once again placed the molds in the refrigerator to harden. The glacé was then complete.

When you make your glacé, allow it a few hours to thoroughly harden—and then all that is left is to eat it. When you're ready, remove the molds from the refrigerator and place them in some warm water for a few seconds to loosen the gel; then invert the dish on a plate, and out will slide your DAUBE GLACÉ. Garnish the serving plate with shredded lettuce. Serve with crackers of your choice. Serves ten to twelve.

*To prepare the stock:*

**10 lbs. cow bones**
**3 qts. water (enough to cover the meat by 2 inches)**
**3 onions, unpeeled, sliced in half**
**1 pod garlic**
**3 ribs celery**

**3 or 4 carrots, peeled and sliced**
**5 or 6 bay leaves**
**1 tbsp. whole peppercorns**
**1 lemon, sliced**
**1 sprig dried thyme (not ground)**

*To prepare the daube:*

**1 6-lb. beef shoulder roast**
**2 onions, sliced**
**1 bell pepper, chopped**
**salt and black pepper to taste**

**1 tsp. allspice**
**½ tsp. cayenne pepper**
**dash Tabasco**
**1 lemon, thinly sliced**
**4 sprigs fresh parsley**

# SAUERBRATEN

Being a very light sleeper, I am usually an early riser. In fact, I'm seldom able to sleep later than dawn. On one very cold morning as I came downstairs, turned the thermostat up, and began to read, my thoughts raced back to the time when I was a young boy, six or seven years old, awakening early in the morning. The bedrooms were cold and there were no themostats to bring in the instant heat. I would slip from under the covers and make my way quickly to the kitchen. We lived in one of those shotgun houses, and so I would pass through two more bedrooms before I reached the kitchen. There the stove was blazing and the warmth filled the kitchen. "Go put your shoes on," Memere or Mamete would command, "or you'll catch cold." So back through the house I'd run, slip on my socks (this would suffice), and back to the kitchen again.

I really believe it was those cold morning visits to the kitchen that ultimately assured my interest in—and love for—cooking. The rest of the house would be quiet, but the kitchen was alive, even that early, with activity. On the stove a pot of water was boiling for the morning coffee. I was always allowed to pour the water over the coffee grounds in the coffee-pot. Petesy, Memere's mockingbird, would be trying out a few songs, and it was my job to keep him well fed. We always kept a whole red pepper in his cage. Memere said that the red pepper made him sing more. When the coffee grinder wasn't in use, I would grind some whole corn and put it in his dish. While Memere was baking biscuits or a coffee cake, Mamete would be cooking a pot of oatmeal or grits and maybe unmolding a cream cheese or two. Sometimes, when there was rice left over from the previous evening's meal, there would be a pot of Riz Au Lait. This was made with boiling milk in which the leftover rice was cooked, along with a little sugar and cinnamon. Sometimes we were treated to a dish of Pain Perdu (Lost Bread) made with the leftover stale bread.

But soon it was time for Pepere and Papete to get up and, of course, before they arose they would have to have their demitasse of *café noir*. Sometimes little Leon was allowed to bring the coffee to them. It was black enough to write with—a small cup of very hot coffee with two or three teaspoonfuls of sugar. What an eye-opener! By this time the whole house was bustling and the early morning kitchen magic was gone for awhile. The stock pot was bubbling on the back of the stove and breakfast was ready for everyone, and so it was time for dressing and off to school. But before I left I would watch closely as Memere would prepare her own version of SAUER-BRATEN.

**4 lbs. beef round or rump, cut into 12 equal portions**
**1 tsp. salt**
**½ tsp. black pepper**
**1 clove garlic, cut in half**
**¼ tsp. powdered cloves**
**2 cups thinly sliced onions**
**2 carrots, minced**
**½ cup chopped celery**

**2 cloves garlic, minced**
**2 cups red wine vinegar**
**3 cups water**
**1 cup flour**
**1 stick butter**
**8 to 10 gingersnaps**
**½ cup finely chopped green onions**

*First, rub the pieces of meat with the salt and black pepper and the cut side of the garlic. Place the meat in a bowl and add the spices and vegetables. Heat the vinegar and water in a pot until hot and then pour this over the meat. After the marinade cools, cover and put in the refrigerator for 48 hours. Stir the marinade and turn the meat twice a day. After the marinating process is complete, remove the meat and dredge with flour. Melt the butter in a skillet and then brown the meat on all sides. In the meantime simmer the marinade in a heavy pot. When the meat is brown, add it to the marinade and allow to cook over moderate heat for 2½ to 3 hours until it is fork-tender.*

*When the sauerbraten has been cooking 2½ hours, break 8 to 10 gingersnaps in small pieces and add to the pot and stir until the snaps are absorbed. When the meat is tender, the heat should be turned off and ½ cup of finely chopped green onions added to the pot. Then cover and allow to stand for 10 minutes before serving. This German Creole treat serves six to eight.*

# TIENT DE BOEUF

The elder bush is indeed an all-weather, horticultural miracle! When I was a boy, it grew like weeds. Wherever there was an open space or vacant lot, you could depend on bush after bush of elder stalks. Never were they in short supply, and if you traveled to the outskirts of the city, into the woody sections, the elder proliferated like a povertyweed.

Let me tell you just why the elder plant was an all-purpose wonder. Just as soon as the plant began to develop its lacy white flowers growing in flat clusters, we began to collect them. Memere used them in a number of ways. The young, tender flowers mixed into a batter and fried made delicious fritters. The buds, just before they opened, could be pickled and used like capers. The flowers, when allowed to dry, went into a tea that was a sure cure for colic.

But the medicinal value of the elder went further. The boiled leaves were used as a poultice. If we had a boil or two in the summer, Mamete would cook a handful of the leaves, wrap them in cheese-cloth, and apply it to the sore spot. In a few days the boil would come to a head.

Even the bark was used. Some of it would be stripped from the stalks and boiled with a little sugar. The resulting syrup could be used to keep you "regular."

When the elderberries ripened to their fullest purple, we would gather them by the bucketful, and the versatility of the berry was astounding. Memere would cook a lot of the berries into a rich, dark, purple jelly. She also made a syrup that was delicious poured over your pancakes or calas. During the season, too, there were at least half a dozen times when we enjoyed slices of elderberry pie. Then, for the *pièce de résistance*, there was that wonderful, homemade elderberry wine, a beautiful color, sweet, and with a bit of a kick.

Ah, but the best is still to come! While Memere and Mamete worked with the buds, flowers, berries, and bark, we used the cane of the elder stalk to make our "popguns." Mother Nature is magnificent in many ways, but the quintessence of this perfection was the way in which she coordinated the elder with the maturing of the fruit of the chinaball tree. It was in the "popgun" that these two forces merged into a delight beyond description for any kid able to make and use his own weapon.

Here's how we did it. A piece of the elder stalk was cut and allowed to dry for a few days. Then, between the joints of the cane, a piece six to eight inches long was cut, stripped, and then hollowed out. There was a center section of the cane that was filled with a pithy substance. You cleaned that out, leaving the cane hollow like a gun barrel. Now, a plunger was made with a piece of wood. The diameter of the plunger was very slightly smaller than the bore of the cane. We usually attached a spool at the end of the plunger, and then the gun was ready.

Next the chinaballs were collected. They were slightly larger than the hole in the cane (I told you nature was wonderful) and so with the plunger the first "ball" was pushed through the gun almost to the other end. The second chinaball was jammed into the back end, and when the plunger was struck with the palm of the hand, it produced a pressure which shot the first chinaball out with terrific velocity.

Just one more note about the elder. Sprigs of it were sometimes pinned to doors and windows to keep out the evil spirits!

Whenever I reflect on the wonders of nature, my mind always brings me into the realm of food—and the wonderful way the Creoles made use of leftovers. Here's another one of Memere's favorites for roast. Memere called it "TIENT DE BOEUF" (which is French and is pronounced "tien da buff" and means "held-over beef" or "leftovers").

**10 thin slices meat or 3 cups chopped meat**
**1 lb. sliced mushrooms**
**6 cloves garlic, finely minced**
**1 onion, finely chopped**
**4 green onions, chopped**

**½ cup bread crumbs plus ¼ cup**
**salt and pepper to taste**
**½ cup dry white wine**
**½ cup beef stock**
**2 tbsp. olive oil**

*Use whatever leftover meat you have on hand. In a bowl mix together the mushrooms, garlic, onion, green onions, ½ cup of the crumbs, and salt and black pepper to taste. Preheat the oven to 375* degrees. Then grease a large baking dish and spread half of the vegetable mixture over the bottom. Spread the meat over the vegetables and cover with the rest of the vegetables. Pour the wine and the stock over the meat and vegetables, then sprinkle with the remaining ¼ cup of bread crumbs. Pour the olive oil over the top of the casserole. Bake 30 minutes for a real leftover treat. Serves four to six.

## CREOLE SPAGHETTI SAUCE

1 cup sliced smoked hot sausage
¾ cup sliced Italian sausage
1 lb. lean ground beef
2 tbsp. butter
1 large onion, chopped
6 cloves garlic, minced
½ bell pepper, chopped
½ cup chopped parsley
1 6-oz. can tomato paste
1 16-oz. can tomato sauce
1 tsp. salt
½ tsp. black pepper
2 tsp. oregano
2 tsp. basil
4 bay leaves
3 cups water
cooked spaghetti

Place sausages in boiling water for 15 minutes. Drain and set aside. In a Dutch oven cook the ground beef over low heat until any fat has rendered out and the meat is brown. Drain off the fat. Add the butter to the meat in the Dutch oven and then the onion, garlic, bell pepper, and parsley. Sauté over moderate heat until the onion is soft. Stir constantly. Then add the sausages, tomato paste, tomato sauce, and all of the seasonings. Now stir in the water and bring the liquid to a simmer. Simmer, partially covered, for 1 to 1½ hours. Serve over boiled spaghetti. Serves four to six.

# LASAGNE BOLOGNESE

*To prepare the white sauce:*

¼ cup butter
¼ cup flour
2½ cups milk

½ cup grated Parmesan
   cheese
salt and pepper to taste

*Melt the butter in a heavy pan over low heat. Sprinkle in the flour and mix well. Cook over very low heat for 3 or 4 minutes, stirring constantly, and then slowly add the milk. When the sauce is smooth, continue to simmer and add the Parmesan cheese, stirring until all the cheese is melted. Add the salt and pepper. Set the sauce aside.*

*To prepare the Bolognese sauce:*

3 tbsp. olive oil
1 lb. lean ground beef
1 onion, finely chopped
2 cloves garlic, minced
4 tbsp. tomato paste
½ cup beef stock

½ cup red wine
pinch nutmeg
salt and pepper to taste
1 cup chopped, fresh
   mushrooms

*Heat the oil in a saucepan and then add the beef, the onion, and the garlic. Sauté over moderate heat until the meat is brown. Now add the tomato paste, stock, wine, nutmeg, salt, and pepper. Mix well and let this mixture simmer for about 20 minutes. At this point, add the mushrooms and cook ten more minutes, then set the sauce aside.*

*To prepare the lasagne:*

3 qts. water
1 tbsp. salt
1 tbsp. olive oil
8 oz. lasagne noodles

White sauce
Bolognese sauce
1 cup grated Parmesan
   cheese

Fill a large pot with the water, bring it to a rapid boil, and add the salt and olive oil. Add the lasagne noodles one at a time, gradually, so as not to slow the boiling. Stir gently to separate the lasagne. Cook uncovered until it is al dente, 10 to 15 minutes. Al dente means that it is resistant to the bite. Test every minute or two until the pasta is ready. Drain the lasagne, rinse with warm water, and then spread the lasagne strips on a damp cloth.

Next, you'll need a large, shallow cooking dish. Butter the dish well and cover the bottom with a layer of the Bolognese sauce. Now alternate with layers of lasagne, white sauce, and Bolognese sauce. Use all the ingredients, ending with the white sauce. Sprinkle a thick layer of Parmesan cheese over the top and then bake in a 350-degree preheated oven for about 20 minutes or until the dish is bubbling and brown. Serves six to eight.

# STUFFED MEAT LOAF

The story that follows is taken from one of Leon's newspaper columns, published in 1980:

Just a week into the New Year and already the delightful, dull monotony of the daily grind is in full swing. That wonderful "life of quiet desperation" is back in the Creole kitchen and everything is back to normal. Oh, it isn't that the frantic, frenetic, furious pace of the holiday season wasn't enjoyable, it's just that now I feel more normal and comfortable. As is customary for most writers, I had thought of trying to do a review of the past year's cooking, but the old memory being what it is I couldn't think of too many things that would be appropriate, and so I abandoned the idea. But then I thought of something else. Why not review the year to come? Only seven days have passed and so I decided to review this year, up to now! It all started on New Year's Eve about a minute before midnight. A few revelers at the party we were attending jumped the gun and started their noisemaking full blast. It was at that moment that my "relative pitch, musical talent" was just about destroyed. Today my ears still ring. Then as I stood to salute the new year, June called to my attention a couple of spots from the salad dressing that had landed in my lap with the comment that "maybe the cleaners will be able to do something with those brand new slacks!" (Ah well, I have great confidence in today's technology.) It was a little later that we found out that Colin, our youngest grandson, had gashed his nose falling off a chair onto a flowerpot. Ten stitches, but he'll recover in the new year and ten will get you five that he'll be back on that same chair trying the same trick again soon. Then there's the resolution kick that everyone gets into come January 1st. Most of my friends are on a weight-loss course, and so, at New Year's Day dinner, I somehow got the idea that I was the only one that looked more like a gourmand than a gourmet. But this situation will be short-lived this year. Human nature being what it is, in another week or so the resolution fervor will have died down. Then we'll be ready to get back to some good Creole cooking, like the STUFFED MEAT LOAF—a dish you'll be proud to serve often.

*To prepare the stuffing:*

¼ cup butter
½ cup finely chopped
  onions
½ bunch green onions,
  finely chopped
1 cup finely chopped celery
½ tsp. black pepper

¼ tsp. cayenne pepper
½ tsp. oregano
1 tbsp. grated Parmesan
  cheese
⅓ cup dry white wine
1½ cups seasoned bread
  crumbs

*Melt the butter in a skillet and add the onions, green onions, and celery. Sauté until the vegetables are soft. Stir in the seasonings, Parmesan cheese, and the wine and simmer for 5 minutes. Remove from the heat, stir in the bread crumbs, and set aside.*

*To prepare the loaf:*

2½ lbs. lean, ground beef
1 egg
½ cup finely chopped
  onions
½ bunch green onions,
  finely chopped
1 tbsp. minced fresh parsley
½ cup milk

½ cup seasoned bread
  crumbs
2 tsp. salt
½ tsp. black pepper
¼ tsp. Tabasco
2 hard-cooked eggs
4 strips bacon

*In a large bowl mix all of the ingredients except the eggs and the bacon. Be sure everything is thoroughly mixed. Now spread the mixture out on a large sheet of waxed paper. Form the mixture into an oval shape about one inch thick. Spread the stuffing over the meat mixture leaving a 2-inch border of meat free of the stuffing. Now place the hard-cooked eggs in line down the center of the oval and roll the meat just as you would a jelly roll. Seal the loaf at both ends and then lay the bacon strips over the top. Transfer the loaf to a shallow baking pan and bake in a preheated 350-degree oven for about an hour.*

*Serve hot or cold, with a béarnaise or other sauce of your choice. Serves six to eight.*

# PANÉED VEAL

This is a traditional veal dish—veal round or cutlet pounded thin, seasoned, dipped in egg, rolled in bread crumbs, and fried golden brown. This is a really old New Orleans kind of cooking. We usually served this with small new potatoes, boiled and buttered with fresh parsley and minced garlic added, along with a green salad and hot French bread.

8 veal cutlets, cut about
⅜-inch thick
salt and pepper to taste
2 eggs, lightly beaten

2 cups Italian bread crumbs
½ cup vegetable oil
8 sprigs fresh parsley
4 slices lemon

*Trim any fat from the veal and remove the skin around the edge. If any skin is left on the cutlet, the meat will curl as it cooks. Cut the veal into 2- by 4-inch pieces and place each piece between sheets of plastic wrap; pound the meat to half their thickness (use a mallet, the flat side of your cleaver, or a rolling pin).*

*Sprinkle both sides with salt and pepper, then dip the pieces of veal first in the eggs and then in the bread crumbs. Coat each piece thoroughly with the crumbs and then shake off the excess. Place the breaded veal on a platter to dry for about 15 or 20 minutes before frying. Do not chill the breaded veal before frying, because this will tend to make it absorb an excess amount of oil.*

*Heat the oil in a heavy sauté pan and fry the veal one to two pieces at a time until golden brown (about 2 minutés on each side). Place the veal on a platter lined with several layers of paper towels, and put it in a preheated 200-degree oven to keep warm. Serve with the parsley and a lemon slice. The addition of a little lemon juice adds to the flavor when eating the cutlets. Serves four.*

# PAPETE'S VEAL STEW

Leon's father loved this veal stew.

1 lb. boneless stew meat
1 lb. veal stew meat (with bone)
4 tbsp. vegetable oil or lard
½ cup flour
2 medium onions, coarsely chopped
6 cloves garlic, minced
6 cups warm water

3 bay leaves
1½ tsp. salt
½ tsp. black pepper
¼ tsp. cayenne pepper
1 tsp. thyme
½ tsp. allspice
4 tbsp. minced, fresh parsley
cooked rice

*In a cast-iron Dutch oven, brown the meat in the oil over moderate heat, turning the meat to brown on all sides. Remove the meat to a platter.*

*Add the flour to the oil and, over moderate heat, stirring constantly, make a dark brown roux. (This could take 20 to 30 minutes. You don't want high heat because you don't want it to burn.) When it is a dark, reddish, brick color add the onions and stir briskly for 2 or 3 minutes over moderate heat, then add the garlic and stir constantly until the onions are soft. Add the warm water and stir until everything is well mixed, then add the bay leaves, salt, peppers, thyme, and allspice. Return the meat to the pot; stir well. Simmer, partially covered, for 1½ to 2 hours, stirring occasionally. Taste to adjust seasonings; add the parsley. Serve over hot, fluffy rice. Serves four to six.*

# KIDNEYS BORDELAISE

We often had covered-dish dinners at our church on Sundays for which Leon would prepare one of his many culinary delights. There were many people in the church who were transplants to New Orleans and classed themselves as finicky eaters. One Sunday Leon prepared what he called "Persian Ragout" and served it over rice. It smelled divine and it tasted terrific! Soon the pot was empty. We sat around and chatted with the folks, and they kept questioning him as to what was in the dish. Needless to say, he kept them in suspense for ages. When he finally told them it was kidney stew, they were shocked—to say the least! With our method of cooking, using the traditional brown roux and wonderful spices, I daresay anything in the world could be turned into a delightful and tasty dish. So here's the recipe for Leon's Persian Ragout (actually, KIDNEYS BORDELAISE).

4 or 5 veal kidneys
3 qts. water
6 tbsp. butter
3 tbsp. flour
½ cup finely chopped green
  onions
3 cloves garlic, minced
½ lb. sliced fresh
  mushrooms
2 cups beef stock
¾ cup red wine

½ tsp. thyme
dash Tabasco
1 tbsp. Worcestershire
  sauce
1 tsp. salt
½ tsp. black pepper
¼ tsp. cayenne pepper
2 tbsp. finely chopped fresh
  parsley
hot cooked rice

*Slice the kidneys and trim off all of the fat. Place the kidneys into boiling water, and when the water returns to a boil, cook for 1 minute. Drain, discard the liquid, and set the kidneys aside in a covered bowl.*

*In a heavy-bottomed Dutch oven melt the butter over moderate heat. When the butter foams, add the flour and, stirring constantly, make a golden-brown roux. Now add the green onions and the garlic and sauté over moderate heat for 2 minutes. Add the* mushrooms and simmer for another minute. Add the beef stock and stir until the sauce is well blended. Add the wine, thyme, Tabasco, Worcestershire sauce, salt, and the black and cayenne pepper. Bring the sauce to a boil, reduce the heat to medium and simmer, partially covered, for 25 minutes until it is reduced by about one-third the quantity.

Add the kidneys to the sauce and bring the mixture to a simmer. Cook, partially covered, for 15 minutes.

Add the parsley and serve over hot, cooked rice, and with hot French bread and a glass of red wine for a meal you won't forget. Serves four to six.

# CHAURICE SAUSAGE

Breathes there a housewife
With soul so dead
That never to herself has said
With autumn's weather so sublime
I guess it's sausage-making time.

(With an apology to all poets who ever set pen to paper)

But of course autumn was the time when the leaves browned and covered the ground and always, on weekends, there would be the smell of burning leaves. And in the kitchen there was a different smell. It was a pungent mix of onion and garlic and thyme and allspice and black and red pepper. The preparation for making sausage started with a trip to the French Market. A marvelous source of the sausages was the black women who made wonderfully seasoned *boudin* and *saucisson*. Their cries of *"mes bons saucissons, mes bonnes saucisses!"* rang out in the neighborhood.

These well-seasoned *boudins* and *saucissons* were the basis for many fine Creole dishes. There were also times when the sausages were eaten as the main dish. They were sometimes cooked in deep fat until they were browned; at other times they were broiled. Another method of preparation was boiling the sausages for about 5 minutes, then draining them and panfrying. But I think the greatest use for sausage was in gumbos and jambalayas.

In making sausage, iceboxes being what they were, the Creole housewife generally prepared a sufficient quantity just for a day or two. What a chaurice Memere would turn out! This was always our favorite. It was the sharpest of all the Creole sausages, and, cooked in a sauce piquante, there was nothing better in the Creole repertoire. There were times when, for a change, Memere would grind out a *boudin blanc*. This was sausage with rice as a filler. The *boudin rouge?* Well, I never knew anyone in the family to try making it. (This was the sausage that started off with hog's blood.) However, Mamete would often buy the blood rings at the French Market and fry them for dinner.

But getting back to the chaurice: first, some good fresh pork had to be found. This was where Memere's expertise shone. She would indicate to the butcher the piece of pork that she wanted to examine, and the meat would be thoroughly inspected. Memere would feel it to be sure it was not getting slimy. Then she would examine its color. Finally it had to pass the nose test! When the meat was deemed fresh enough, it was purchased for the sausage. Memere would usually start with 4 pounds of very lean, fresh pork, together with 2 pounds of fresh fat pork.

| | |
|---|---|
| **2 lbs. fresh pork fat** | **3 tsp. salt** |
| **4 lbs. lean, fresh pork** | **1 tsp. thyme** |
| **2 cups minced onions** | **2 tbsp. minced parsley** |
| **4 cloves garlic, minced** | **2 bay leaves, finely minced** |
| **2 tsp. cayenne pepper** | **½ tsp. powdered allspice** |
| **1 tsp. chili powder** | **15 ft. pig casings (purchase** |
| **2 tsp. black pepper** | **at a butcher supply house)** |

*Let me make one point here: never did we use ground pork. The meat was bought in one chunk, carefully cut into smaller pieces, then hashed with cleavers or sharp knives until the consistency was like ground meat. The difference, as Memere explained it, was that* this way all of the meat juices were not squeezed out, which would have happened if the meat had been ground. So after the meat was chopped into very small pieces, it was combined with all the rest of the ingredients and mixed thoroughly. This mixing part was very important, and it usually took an hour or so to be sure that the mixture was completely homogenized.

Now came the fun part. The "sausage attachment" was clamped on to the front of the meat grinder and the casing was slipped on to the end. The casings for the sausage were made of pig entrails and had to be thoroughly washed before being used.

(The casings can be purchased at a butcher supply house. They are packaged in salt, so you must soak the casings in cool water for 5 or 6 hours. Every 15 to 20 minutes, pour out the water and replace with fresh water. Then open the casing at one end—much as if you were putting water in a balloon, only the casings are open on both ends— and let the cool fresh water run through the length of the casing.)

The meat mixture was fed into the grinder and pushed way into the sausage casing. After each link, about 3 to 4 inches in length, the casing was knotted; each link was between two knots when we completed the task of stuffing. It was always my job (by choice, of course) to turn the handle of the grinder. So in a short time, some of the area's best Creole chaurice was in the icebox. For dinner that evening it didn't take Memere long to smother a pot of cabbage. With a length of browned, crisp chaurice on the side, who could ask for a better treat?

# HOGSHEAD CHEESE

I wax nostalgic when I remember the time that the whole family, Leon, Chris, Yvette, David, and I, went on an excursion to Leon's father's home early one Saturday morning. Our help had been solicited for a family project embarked upon only three or four times a year—the making of hogshead cheese. Hogshead cheese is really a misnomer, because it does not actually contain dairy products. It is a congealed mixture of cooked meat and finely chopped seasonings.

Leon's father had just retired from an administrative job. He was a very fastidious gentleman, even to the point of eating fresh apples or pears with a knife and fork! When we arrived, this was the scene: Memere was the *la directrice* (the director) and Papete (Leon's father) was standing over a soup kettle with a slotted spoon in hand. As we came in, he said, "Can you believe I've come to this? I'm fishing the pig's teeth out as we boil the hogshead." He tried to sound perturbed, but he had a twinkle in his eye.

Soon Memere had all of us busy chopping meat or seasonings to go in the hogshead cheese. It took us all day, but there was always a spirit of fun and adventure. Finally, we had the great joy of eating this delicacy. It was most often used as an appetizer, served on small slices of French bread. There was usually a bountiful supply to share with family, friends, and neighbors.

*To prepare the meat:*

**1 hog's head, cleaned and
    quartered
6 pig's feet
3-lb. pork roast (Boston
    Butt)**

**2 onions, quartered
3 tsp. salt
1 lemon, sliced**

*First, have the butcher clean and quarter the hog's head. This means he has removed the brains, eyes, ears, and tongue. Soak the quarters about 6 hours in cold water to extract the blood. Also wash the pig's feet thoroughly. Put the hog's head, pig's feet, pork roast, onions, salt and lemon into a heavy 6- to 8-quart pot and add* enough cold water to cover the pork by 2 inches. Bring the liquid to a boil, then reduce heat to a simmer. Cook for 3½ to 4 hours or until the meat begins to fall off the bone. Drain and reserve the stock. Remove the hog's head, pig's feet, and the pork roast, and finely chop the meat. Discard the fat and the bones. When the stock is cool, refrigerate it so that the fat will rise to the top. Remove the grease and simmer the liquid until it is reduced to about one-third of its original quantity.

*To prepare the cheese:*

**1 onion, finely chopped**
**1 bunch green onions, finely chopped**
**2 ribs celery, finely chopped**
**3 tbsp. minced garlic**
**1 tsp. freshly ground black pepper**
**½ tsp. cayenne pepper**
**½ tsp. chili powder**
**½ tsp. allspice**

**3 whole bay leaves**
**1 tsp. thyme**
**1 tbsp. lemon juice**
**1 cup Madeira wine**
**4 tbsp. Worcestershire sauce**
**⅓ cup minced fresh parsley**
**½ cup finely chopped green onions**

Now put all the chopped meat and the above ingredients, except for the parsley and the ½ cup green onions, into the stock pot with the remaining liquid. Simmer over moderate heat for 45 minutes to one hour, stirring occasionally, until the liquid is reduced by about one-third. Now taste to adjust the salt and pepper, especially the latter. Creole hogshead cheese is meant to be hot with pepper. Add enough cayenne pepper for your throat to be warmed thoroughly as you test it. Pour into several sizes of ungreased containers to suit your particular needs. Then cover with plastic wrap and refrigerate for at least 6 hours.

When ready to serve, unmold and serve with crackers or French bread. Serves eight to ten.

# CROWN ROAST OF PORK

**Pork crown roast, about 12
ribs (allow 2 ribs per
person)**

**salt and pepper
aluminum foil**

*Preheat the oven to 450 degrees. Wipe the roast with a damp cloth, then sprinkle it lightly with salt and pepper. Protect the ends of the bones by wrapping the ends with aluminum foil. Place the roast in the oven and reduce the heat to 350 degrees. Cook 30 minutes per pound.*

*One hour before the roast is done, remove it from the oven and fill the center with Apple-Sausage Dressing (see below) or Cornbread Dressing (see index). Return the roast to the oven and complete the cooking (the internal temperature of the roast should be 185 degrees).*

*To prepare the gravy:*

**2 tbsp. flour
2 cups liquid (½ water and ½
stock or wine)**

*Remove the roast from the pan. Pour off all but 2 tablespoons of the drippings. Add the flour to the pan and stir with a wire whisk until the flour and the drippings are well combined and smooth. Scrape the bottom of the pan to loosen any particles of meat or seasonings. Add the liquid and blend until smooth. Cook for 3 minutes, and then pour into a warm serving bowl. Keep the gravy warm and serve with the roast. Serves six.*

*Note: Peeled sweet potatoes can be placed in the roasting pan during the last hour of cooking. They are delicious this way. Glazed onions are another good accompaniment for a superb company dinner.*

# APPLE-SAUSAGE DRESSING

1 lb. ground pork
½ cup finely chopped onion
¼ cup finely chopped green
  onions
1 clove garlic, minced
1 cup chopped celery
2 cups peeled and diced
  apples

1 tsp. salt
¼ tsp. paprika
¼ tsp. cayenne pepper
4 cups soft bread cubes
¼ cup minced fresh parsley

Sauté the ground pork in a skillet over moderate heat. Drain all but 2 tablespoons of the drippings, then add the next 8 ingredients into the skillet. Cook over moderate heat, stirring frequently, until the onions and celery are soft. Remove from the heat.

Place the bread cubes and parsley in a large mixing bowl and add the sautéed pork mixture. Stir thoroughly. The stuffing is now ready for the roast.

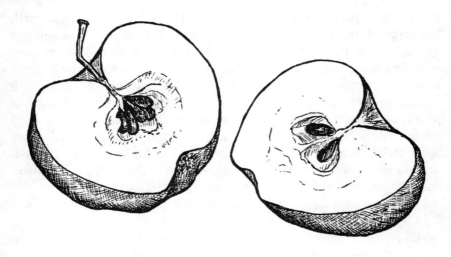

# PORK CHOPS BRAISED IN FRESH TOMATO SAUCE

Memere had a few beliefs and practices that, come Hades or floods, could not be changed. One was her attitude toward canned foods. No way could she ever be convinced to use anything canned. Her belief was that the metal, no matter how clean or sterilized, contaminated anything packed inside. In later years she made a couple of concessions to tomato paste and condensed milk, but that was as far as she ever bent. Her ideas about vegetables were just as strict. A vegetable had to be demonstrably fresh, otherwise she eschewed it like the plague. Even slightly wilted lettuce, celery, or peppers were not for her. When the gumbo of the day was okra, the okra were severely tested. They were culled from the bin one by one, and before she bagged them she would hold one in her hand with the pointed end up. With her thumb she would bend the okra at the tip. If the tip popped off, she knew it was fresh and tender. If the tip bent over limply there was no okra gumbo that day.

But it was in her shopping for meat and cheese that she was most precise and particular. A piece of prepackaged meat? She would have had the housewife's hissy at the very suggestion! In her mind there was never a thought of buying meat that had been precut. First, the large chunk of meat from which she might eventually buy her steak, chops, or roast had to be closely examined. The butcher would remove the skewers from the large piece and bring it close for Memere's inspection. It was poked, stroked, and smelled, and if the quality was up to her standard, the butcher was told how to cut her particular portion. After the meat was sliced it was trimmed of its fatty border (Memere would insist on this), and then it was weighed. After the butcher had wrapped the meat, it was further wrapped in a slightly dampened towel before it went into the basket. This was done to protect its freshness, she explained.

Memere was just as finicky when she purchased cheese. She would insist that air destroyed the flavor of cheese and so, after she purchased a chunk of cheese, it too was carefully wrapped in a piece of oilcloth which was brought along for that express purpose, and so it was, home from the market with the ingredients for dinner—pork chops. Now for you lovers of pork chops (and who isn't one?), here's a real Creole treat, PORK CHOPS BRAISED IN FRESH TOMATO SAUCE. It's a rather imposing list of ingredients, but a recipe well worth the trouble.

**6 center-cut pork chops, about ½ inch thick**
**1½ cups sliced onions**
**1 cup sliced carrots**
**2 bay leaves**
**¼ tsp. thyme**
**½ tsp. basil**
**¼ tsp. cloves**
**1 tbsp. minced parsley**
**½ tsp. salt**
**½ tsp. black pepper**
**1 pt. dry white wine**

**3 tbsp. vegetable oil**
**3 tbsp. butter**
**1 cup minced white onions**
**2 tbsp. flour**
**2 cups ripe tomatoes, peeled, seeded, and sliced**
**2 cloves garlic, minced**
**2 tbsp. tomato paste**
**2 tbsp. chopped, fresh basil or 1 tbsp. dried basil**

*First, marinate the pork chops in a dish in a mixture of all the ingredients down to and including the wine. Let this marinate for several hours in the refrigerator, turning a few times. When ready to cook, remove the chops from the marinade and cook the marinade in a covered saucepan over low heat for 45 minutes. Strain the sauce and set it aside. (You won't be using the vegetables.)*

*Dry the chops well, and brown them in the oil on both sides. Now pour out the fat, add the butter and the white onions, and sauté for about 10 minutes over low heat. Sprinkle the flour over the chops and simmer for 5 minutes longer. Stir in the tomatoes and garlic, cover the skillet, and simmer for another 5 minutes. Now add the cooked marinade and the tomato paste and cook a few minutes longer.*

*At this point arrange the chops in a baking dish or casserole, pour the sauce over them, cover and bake in a preheated 325-degree oven for 30 minutes. To serve, arrange the chops on a serving platter, pour the sauce over them, and sprinkle with the basil. Serves six.*

# ROAST SUCKLING PIG

One Easter, we celebrated by having an Easter Vigil at my church. Following an ancient Christian tradition, we began the celebration at dawn on Easter morning with a beautiful service in the church. About 8:00 A.M. we gathered in the parish hall for a sumptuous breakfast. The early Christians would have feasted on lamb, but had they lived in southwest Louisiana, we decided, a suckling pig should have been their choice—and it was definitely ours!

The pig we purchased weighed about 25 pounds. (There is not that much meat on a suckling pig, so to serve a large crowd, a fresh leg of pork is a necessary addition. Note: a pig weighing more than 12 to 15 pounds will not fit in an ordinary oven. We used a commercial oven to bake ours.) The pig had to bake over eight hours. The meat was sweet and succulent, the dressing a mélange of wonderful aromas and tastes, and the skin crisp and oh, so good!

After it was cooked, we dressed the golden-brown, gleaming, glistening pig in a festive manner—with Gerber daisies for eyes and a garland of daisies around its neck; the platter was garnished with greens and vegetables galore. It was a very dramatic moment when this elegant and beautiful dish was carried into the room—a joyous climax to our celebration of our Easter feast which marked the end of Lenten fasting!

*To prepare the pig:*

**1 12- to 15-lb. pig**
**2 tsp. salt**
**1 tsp. black pepper**

**½ tsp. cayenne pepper**
**1 tbsp. paprika**
**3 tbsp. oil**

*Additional supplies:*

**aluminum foil**
**1 apple**

**Garnish: parsley, radishes, cherry tomatoes, mushrooms, bibb lettuce, and fresh flowers**

Have the butcher thoroughly clean the pig and remove the eyeballs. (This is necessary because they will burst during cooking.) Thoroughly rinse the pig inside and out and pat dry with toweling. Mix the salt, black pepper, cayenne pepper, and paprika together and season the inside of the pig. Rub the oil generously over the body of the pig. Make a second batch of the salt, black pepper, cayenne pepper, and paprika and sprinkle over the body of the pig. Now the pig is ready to be stuffed.

*To prepare the stuffing:*

1 lb. ground pork
1 lb. ground beef
2 large onions, coarsely chopped
1 large bell pepper, coarsely chopped
3 ribs celery, coarsely chopped
4 cloves garlic, minced
1 bunch green onions, finely chopped

2 medium sweet potatoes, peeled and coarsely chopped
1 medium eggplant, coarsely chopped
3 apples, peeled and coarsely chopped
1 tsp. salt
2 tsp. black pepper
½ tsp. cayenne pepper
3 bay leaves

Mix all the ingredients together in a large bowl. The stuffing is not cooked—all of the meat and vegetables are raw. It is now ready to be stuffed loosely inside of the pig. Any extra stuffing can be baked separately in a casserole dish in a 325-degree oven for 3 hours. With a needle and thread sew the cavity of the pig. Place the pig in a large pan, point the back feet forward and tuck the front feet under. Cut a triangle of aluminum foil and cover the ears; also cover the tail with foil. Roll up a wad of foil and put it into the mouth of the pig to hold it open. (Later you will replace the foil with an apple.) Bake in a preheated 325-degree oven for about 4 to 5 hours. Every 20 minutes, baste the pig with the juice collected in the bottom of the baking pan. When a meat thermometer reaches 180 to 185 degrees and the thigh meat is tender when pressed and the legs move in their sockets, then the pig is done. Remove pan from oven and let the roast pig stand at least 15 to 20 minutes. Place the golden pig on a large platter or plank of wood covered with foil. Place daisies in the eye openings and make a garland of daisies to place around its neck. Replace the foil in the mouth with a red apple. Garnish the serving tray. Let the pig be admired before carving. When you are ready to serve, remove the thread and spoon out the stuffing into a serving bowl. Carve the meat and be sure to serve pieces of the crispy pig's skin. Serves eight.

## PORK ROAST AND SMOTHERED CABBAGE

4-lb. end-cut pork roast
2 tbsp. oil
1 large onion, coarsely
  chopped
2½ cups water
1 tsp. salt
1 tbsp. Worcestershire
  sauce

½ tsp. thyme
½ tsp. black pepper
¼ tsp. cayenne pepper
¼ tsp. Tabasco
3 lbs. fresh cabbage
4 medium potatoes, peeled
  and quartered

Brown the pork roast in oil in a cast-iron Dutch oven over moderate heat. Put the roast on a plate, then remove all but 1 tablespoon of oil from the pot. Add the onion to the Dutch oven and brown lightly. Add the water and seasonings. When the water boils, return the roast to the pot and reduce the heat to simmer. Cover and cook for 1½ hours. Check every 15 or 20 minutes and add more water if neccssary.

Cut the cabbage into small wedges; rinse them in cold water. Place the cabbage wedges around the roast in the Dutch oven; cook over low heat for ½ hour. Add the potatoes and simmer for 20 minutes or until the potatoes are tender. Serves six.

Note: We serve this meal with French bread or corn bread to absorb every drop of the delicious broth (which we call Pot Likker).

# SAUSAGE, HAM, AND CHICKEN JAMBALAYA

4 tbsp. vegetable oil
1 lb. andouille sausage, sliced ¼-inch thick
½ lb. chaurice sausage, cut in small dice
1 lb. ham, diced
1 3-lb. fryer, cut up and seasoned with salt and pepper
1 tbsp. brown sugar
2 cups coarsely chopped onions
1 cup coarsely chopped celery
1 medium bell pepper, coarsely chopped
3 cloves garlic, minced
1 tbsp. paprika
1 16-oz. can tomatoes, chopped
5 cups chicken stock
2 bay leaves
1 tsp. basil
1½ tsp. salt (may need 2 tsp.)
2 to 3 drops Tabasco
½ tsp. cayenne pepper
½ tsp. black pepper
2½ cups raw rice (Uncle Ben's Converted)
1 bunch green onions, finely chopped
½ cup minced fresh parsley

*Pour the oil into a large, heavy iron pot and heat. Add the andouille sausage and lightly brown over moderate heat. Remove the andouille from the pot, add the chaurice and the ham, lightly brown, remove it from the pot, and set aside.*

*Season the chicken lightly with salt and black pepper. Brown the chicken, then remove it from the pot. Add the brown sugar and over moderate heat stir constantly for about 2 minutes. The brown sugar is used for color and taste. While stirring, it will smell like burning sugar, but do not let it burn or turn black. Now add the onions, celery, and the bell pepper. Cook over moderate heat, stirring until the vegetables are tender. Add the garlic and paprika; stir constantly. Now add the tomatoes, the stock, bay leaves, basil, salt, Tabasco, cayenne pepper, black pepper, the chicken, ham and sausage. Bring all of this to a boil, reduce the heat, cover, and simmer for 45 minutes. Taste to adjust seasonings. Next add the rice, stirring well. Bring back to a boil, then reduce the heat, cover,* and simmer over low heat for 25 to 30 minutes. Add the green onions and parsley and stir, turning the jambalaya from top to bottom. Remove from the heat and let set for 5 minutes. Serves eight to ten.

## STUFFED PORK CHOPS

3 tbsp. butter
1 cup finely chopped celery
½ cup finely chopped green onions
1½ cups soft bread cubes
2 tbsp. minced fresh parsley
½ tsp. salt
1 apple, peeled, cored, and diced

1 tbsp. white wine plus ⅓ cup
6 rib pork chops, 1½ inches thick (have the butcher cut a pocket through the lean part to the bone of each chop)
3 tbsp. vegetable oil
⅓ cup water

Melt the butter in a skillet. Add the celery and green onions and cook until tender. Add the bread, parsley, salt, apple, and the 1 tablespoon of wine; mix well to combine. Fill the pockets of the chops with this stuffing and fasten with skewers or toothpicks.

Heat the oil in a large, heavy frying pan over moderate heat. Sprinkle the chops lightly with salt and pepper and fry slowly one or two at a time. As they cook, enough fat will render out to keep the pan greased. Spoon off excess fat if necessary. Brown the chops evenly on both sides and place in a large baking pan.

Remove all but one tablespoon of the fat and add ⅓ cup water and ⅓ cup white wine. Over low heat scrape all the brown bits from the bottom of the pan. Pour this mixture over the chops in the baking pan.

Cover the pan and bake in a preheated 350-degree oven for 45 to 60 minutes. Turn the chops and baste them after 20 minutes. At the end of 45 minutes check the meat to be sure it's fork-tender. Keep loosely covered until ready to serve. Serves six.

Note: Henri's Patates Douces Frites (see index) are a good accompaniment for these pork chops.

# POPSI'S IRISH STEW

My father, Edward St. Ceran Thompson, was of Scotch-Irish background. My children called my dad "Popsi." I lovingly dedicate this recipe to him.

½ cup flour
½ tsp. salt
½ tsp. black pepper
¼ tsp. cayenne pepper
1½ to 2 lbs. lamb stew meat, cut into 1-inch cubes
3 tbsp. oil
1 large onion, coarsely chopped
1 small bell pepper, coarsely chopped
2 ribs celery, coarsely chopped
2 cloves garlic, minced
¼ tsp. thyme

1 bay leaf
½ tsp. black pepper
½ tsp. salt
¼ tsp. cayenne pepper
2 cups beef stock
3 dashes Tabasco
6 to 8 small white onions, peeled
6 carrots, cut into 1 inch pieces
½ lb. fresh mushrooms, quartered if medium size, sliced if large
2 tbsp. butter
3 tbsp. minced fresh parsley

Mix the flour, salt, and black and cayenne peppers together. Roll the meat (I ask my butcher for lamb stew and he uses the shoulder or the leg of lamb) in this mixture. In a heavy Dutch oven, fry the meat in the oil until it is brown. Remove and set aside. Add the onion, bell pepper, and celery and cook over moderate heat, stirring constantly, until the onion is almost transparent. Add the garlic and continue to stir until you can smell the garlic; then add the thyme, bay leaf, black pepper, salt, cayenne pepper, the stock, and Tabasco. Simmer over low heat for about 2 hours. Stir occasionally. If the liquid evaporates, add a little more stock; the meat should be just barely covered.

After about 1½ hours of cooking, add the white onions and carrots and continue to simmer until the vegetables are tender. Sauté the mushrooms in the butter and add them to the stew 5 minutes before serving. Add the parsley, adjust the salt and pepper. Serve over cooked rice. Serves four to six.

## MEMERE'S RABBIT STEW

1 2½- to 3-lb. rabbit
salt and black pepper
3 tbsp. butter
2 tbsp. oil
1 large onion, finely
 chopped
4 green onions, finely
 chopped
½ cup celery, finely
 chopped
½ medium bell pepper,
 finely chopped
2 cloves garlic, minced
4 tbsp. flour

2 fresh tomatoes, peeled
 and chopped or 1 16-oz.
 can tomatoes
1½ cups thinly sliced fresh
 mushrooms
1 cup dry white wine
1 cup chicken broth
2 bay leaves
½ tsp. dried thyme
1 tsp. dried tarragon
¼ tsp. cayenne pepper
½ tsp. black pepper
2 tbsp. minced fresh parsley

Cut the rabbit into serving pieces and sprinkle with salt and pepper.

In a heavy pot, heat the butter and oil and fry the rabbit until it is brown on all sides. Remove the meat and set aside. Add the onion, green onions, celery, and bell pepper and cook over moderate heat, stirring constantly, until the onions are almost transparent. Add the garlic and continue to cook, stirring constantly, until you can smell the garlic. Sprinkle the flour into the pot and mix well, stirring constantly. Add the tomatoes, the mushrooms, the wine, and the chicken broth stirring until everything in the sauce is well mixed. Add the bay leaves, thyme, tarragon, and cayenne and black pepper. Stir well. Return the meat to the pot. Bring the liquid to a boil and then reduce the heat to a low simmer and cook for 1½ hours stirring occasionally. Check to see if the rabbit is tender. Pierce the leg with a fork to test doneness. Add the parsley and serve over cooked rice or mashed potatoes. Serves four to six.

# ROAST LEG OF VENISON

In the wooded areas around New Orleans, deer hunting is a popular sport. We have a long, hot summer that ensures a bountiful supply of wild vines and berries and this is what the deer like to eat. It has been claimed that the flavor of the venison brought from the woods in our environs equals or surpasses that of any region of the country. We consider ourselves very lucky to have the opportunity to taste this delicious venison.

My family does not hunt, so the only way I have deer is when a friend like Rick Forstall generously shares part of his bounty. When I have been presented with a leg of venison, then I prepare it as he does.

*To prepare the marinade:*

**2 cups red wine**
**1 large onion, chopped**
**2 large carrots, chopped**
**⅓ cup coarsely chopped, fresh parsley**
**4 whole cloves**
**1 tsp. thyme**
**1 tsp. basil**

**½ tsp. rosemary**
**½ tsp. sugar**
**1 tsp. salt**
**1 tsp. black pepper**
**½ tsp. cayenne pepper**
**2 cloves garlic**
**¾ cup olive oil**

*Mix all of the marinade ingredients and set aside for the moment.*

*To prepare the venison:*

**5- to 6-lb. leg of venison**

*Place the venison in a large kettle of cold water. Venison is rather bloody, so change the water every 15 minutes for 1 hour. At the end of this time place the roast in a stainless steel or enamelware pot and add the marinade. Refrigerate the venison in the marinade for 24 hours. Then remove the meat from the marinade and pat it dry. Strain the marinade and set aside.*

*To prepare the roast:*

**5 or 6 cloves garlic, thinly
   sliced**
**2 tbsp. olive oil**
**salt and black pepper**
**1 tsp. cayenne pepper**
**2 lbs. slab bacon or a slab of
   fat from the butcher's
   shop**

**½ cup red currant jelly**
**½ cup red wine**
**1 tbsp. flour**
**1 tbsp. brandy**

Insert the cloves of garlic deep into the flesh of the roast. Brush with olive oil and sprinkle with salt and pepper.

Cut the salt pork or slab bacon in strips. Or do as I do—I ask my butcher for some slabs of fat which he has trimmed from other cuts of meat. Cover the meat with whatever fat you choose and loop string around the meat, crosswise and lengthwise, as you would tie up a parcel. (When the deer is shot and dressed, all of the fat is removed as it can become rancid very quickly; therefore, the meat needs some other fat to avoid being dry.)

Place the meat fat side up on a rack in a baking pan. Place 1 cup of strained marinade in the pan and baste frequently throughout the roasting. Roast uncovered in a 350-degree oven for 35 to 40 minutes per pound. Approximately 30 minutes before the roast is done, remove the fat covering the meat so that the roast can brown.

Remove the roast to a platter, and drain all but 1 tablespoon of juice from the pan. Place the pan on the burners. In the pan slowly melt the currant jelly and blend with the drippings. Add the wine and stir well. When the gravy has thickened a little, sprinkle in the flour and whisk; make sure there are no lumps. Cook at least 2 to 3 minutes. Add the brandy, mix well, and pour the sauce into a bowl or gravy boat to be served with the roast. Serves eight.

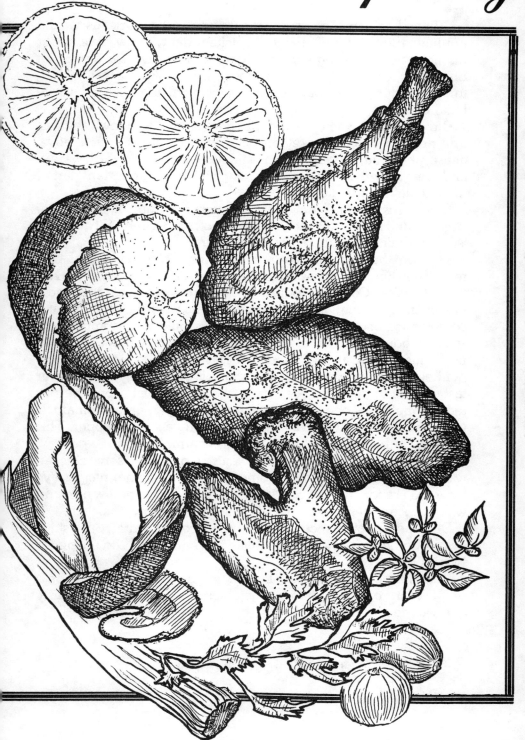

When Leon and I were growing up here in New Orleans, we did not have the bountiful supply of chicken that we now have in our markets. So it was a great treat to have a chicken for dinner on Sunday, and a turkey, duck, or goose for a holiday meal. In fact, turkey, stuffed and roasted to a rich brown crust, is still our favorite holiday meal.

But when a Creole cook described an animal as a fowl, she was referring not only to turkey and chicken, but also to duck, dove, geese, pheasant, squab, quail, or wild turkey, many of which were— and are—abundant in this area. They became an important part of the Creole family's diet.

Chicken is plentiful now. It is a favorite in farm kitchens, city kitchens and restaurant kitchens. The cook's most frequent question is, How shall I cook the chicken tonight?

I am sure that you will enjoy the recipe for "Chicken Carnival." Let me tell you how this recipe came to be. Leon decided to enter the National Chicken Cooking Contest. (Yes, there is such a contest, and it has been held annually for over 30 years.) He thought that the combination of chicken and pork sausage would be very appetizing, so he deboned chicken breasts and rolled each of them around a pork sausage link. These baked in our favorite sauce piquante could not help but be one of the tastiest morsels of food anyone has ever tasted. The ingredients used in "Chicken Carnival" combine our most popular flavors: onion, celery, bell pepper, garlic, tomatoes, wine, lemon juice, bay leaves, thyme, and cayenne pepper. This recipe won Leon a place in the South-central Region.

Because chicken is so versatile, we use it often. We serve chicken with nuts, as in Chicken Amandine. Some of the other recipes I've included are for chicken cooked with cream, mushrooms, rice, and walnuts. And then there's the all-time favorite—fried chicken.

Duck and quail dishes are also great local favorites. And since frozen domestic goose is available, I have included the recipe for Roast Goose.

Whether poultry is cooked in wine or golden-brown gravy, or is prepared in combination with vegetables or nutmeats, it will be tasty and well received.

# WALNUT CHICKEN

One aspect of Memere's cooking that I have never discussed up to now was her occasional deviation into the culinary ways of the Orient—or to be more specific into Chinese cooking. These forays into Chinese cuisine were brought about by her occasional contact with M'sieu Boudin. First I must explain that Memere's knowledge of cooking had been accumulated through kitchen experience. I don't believe I ever saw her reading a cookbook. In fact, there wasn't one in the house. But she talked about food to anyone who listened, and, of course, this led to a great deal of information being exchanged. I have written previously how, since we lived in a predominantly Italian neighborhood, Memere had gleaned so many wonderful Italian family recipes that we enjoyed at our table.

But who, you ask, was M'sieu Boudin? M'sieu Boudin was Chinese and the owner of a Chinese laundry in our neighborhood. It was to his laundry, once a week or so, that Memere would bring a few pieces to be "done": shirt collars to be washed, starched, and ironed, or some particularly fancy work that had to be laundered professionally. It was during these trips to M'sieu's establishment that Memere would swap recipes. Now whether M'sieu Boudin ever cooked Creole I am not able to say, but I do know that Memere wasted not this knowledge she acquired, and we could usually count on a hot and sour soup, sweet and sour pork, or maybe even a won ton treat following a laundry visit. But again, you might ask, a Chinese laundryman with a name like M'sieu Boudin? By way of explanation, allow me a brief digression. I remember, many years ago, at a time when I was thoroughly engrossed with the stories of Mark Twain, an amusing account of a schoolmaster who was teaching a lesson in Greek mythology. I believe the incident is in *The Adventures of Tom Sawyer*. This teacher was relating the story of Icarus. Now Icarus, as you will recall, was the character who wanted to fly. In his enthusiasm he attached a pair of wings to his back and was able to float through the air with the greatest of ease. Ah, but his ambition proved to be his downfall, because Icarus flew so high that the sun melted the wax he had used to attach the wings to his shoulderblades and he fell into the Eridanus and was drowned. Where was the Eridanus? The schoolmaster immediately proclaimed it to be the ancient name of the Erie Canal, and he proved it thusly: Erie Canal, the Eriedrain, the Eriedrainus, consequently, Eridanus! And that's how M'sieu Boudin got his name. First, his real name was Choy Lee. This, with a Chinese accent, sounded like Chau Ree. With a little bit of imagination, it became chaurice, a famous Creole sausage, and from there to Boudin—a name Mr. Lee was stuck with forevermore! But let's leave the M'sieu and sample Memere's adaptations of his recipe for WALNUT CHICKEN.

**6 chicken breast halves, deboned**
**3 tbsp. soy sauce**
**⅓ cup dry sherry or dry white wine**
**2 tsp. sugar**
**½ tsp. salt**
**3 cloves garlic, minced**
**2 ¼-inch thin slices fresh ginger, peeled and minced**

**1 cup sliced onion**
**1 cup coarsely broken walnuts**
**1 cup celery, bias-cut**
**3 tbsp. vegetable oil**
**1¼ cups chicken broth**
**⅔ cup bamboo shoots, drained**
**⅔ cup water chestnuts, sliced**
**cooked rice**

*To prepare the sauce:*

**1 tsp. sugar**
**1 tbsp. cornstarch**

**2 tbsp. sherry**

*Remove the skin from the deboned, raw chicken and cut the meat lengthwise into very thin strips. Mix the soy sauce, sherry, sugar, salt, garlic, and ginger for the marinade; pour over the chicken and mix it very well. Refrigerate for at least 30 minutes, turning the chicken over in the marinade every ten minutes.*

*Slice the onion in rings, separate rings and cut the celery in ⅓-inch pieces.*

In a skillet toast the walnuts in hot oil, stirring constantly. Remove the walnuts and drain on paper towels.

Remove the chicken from the marinade and fry the chicken over moderately high heat. Using two forks, toss the strips around the pan to keep it moving so that it cooks thoroughly but does not burn. This will take 5 or 6 minutes. Remove the chicken.

Add the onion, celery, and ½ cup of the chicken broth to the skillet. Cook uncovered for 5 to 10 minutes or until the onion is soft.

Combine the ingredients for the sauce and mix well with the remaining chicken broth and then add this to the skillet with the onion and celery. Cook until the sauce thickens, over moderately high heat, stirring constantly. Then add the chicken, bamboo shoots, water chestnuts, and walnuts. Heat thoroughly. Serve over cooked rice. Serves four to six.

# CHICKEN CARNIVAL

This won Leon kudos from friends and you too, will win many accolades for this great-tasting recipe!

*To prepare the chicken:*

**8 chicken breast halves**
**8 links breakfast pork**
  **sausage**
**salt and pepper**
**2 tbsp. butter**

**2 tbsp. vegetable oil**
**½ cup finely chopped green**
  **onions**
**3 tbsp. finely chopped fresh**
  **parsley**

*Cut the chicken breasts in half; skin and debone them. Place the deboned breasts between two pieces of wax paper and pound the meat with a mallet, a rolling pin, or the flat side of a meat cleaver. Pound the meat hard until it covers nearly twice the area. Place a link of the sausage on each breast and bring edges together, making the breast conform to the shape of the sausage. Secure with a toothpick. Salt and pepper each chicken-sausage roll. In a heavy Dutch oven sauté the chicken in the butter and oil until it is lightly browned. As they brown remove the chicken from the pan and drain on paper towels. Use the same saucepan to make the sauce. Place in a baking dish and add the sauce.*

*To prepare the sauce:*

2 tbsp. butter
2 tbsp. drippings left in saucepan from frying
4 tbsp. flour
2 cups finely chopped onion
1 cup finely chopped celery
1 cup finely chopped bell pepper
2 cloves garlic, minced
1 16-oz. can tomatoes, coarsely chopped
1 cup chicken stock
2 tbsp. red wine

1 cup water
1½ tsp. lemon juice
2 thin slices lemon
¾ tsp. salt
½ tsp. cayenne pepper
½ tsp. black pepper
1 tsp. basil
½ tsp. thyme
2 bay leaves
½ cup finely chopped green onions
3 tbsp. finely chopped fresh parsley

Use the Dutch oven you used to brown the chicken. Pour out all but 2 tablespoons of the drippings from the chicken and sausage; add the butter. When oil and butter are heated add the flour. Cook over moderate heat, stirring constantly, until you have a medium dark-brown roux. Watch this carefully and stir constantly. Add the onion, celery, and bell pepper and simmer, stirring constantly, until the onions are almost transparent. Now add the garlic and stirring constantly, simmer for about 3 or 4 minutes. Add the tomatoes, and stir to mix all ingredients, continuing to simmer for about 5 minutes. Now add the rest of the ingredients except for the green onions and parsley. Mix well and simmer slowly, partially covered, for about 45 minutes. Your sauce is now ready to add to the Chicken Carnival. Bake in a 350-degree oven for 30 to 40 minutes. Five minutes before the chicken is finished baking, add the green onions and parsley.

Serve, if you wish, over hot fluffy rice. Serves six to eight.

# RICE AND CREOLE CHICKEN

In today's frenetic world there are certain indicators or "bellwethers" that, if carefully watched, seem to act as a gauge for our economy—or so I'm told. When they're up, prosperity; when down, recession. Now Memere had an indicator that she stoutly maintained gave her an infallible guide to a person's cooking expertise. To her it was a simple maxim: "Show me how you cook your rice and I'll know what kind of cook you are." Ah, the arrogance of culinary genius!

But seriously, dear reader, those old Creole cooks were virtuosi when it came to turning out a pot of rice for their beans or gumbos. They knew exactly how to pet and pamper it to a state of fluffy perfection. They started off with long-grain rice (the short or mid-grain rices are more glutinous which makes them next to impossible to cook to a white fluffiness). The long-grain rice was washed until the water covering it was perfectly clear. This sometimes required as many as five or six washings. To further remove the starch, the rice was rubbed between the hands while still in the water. Then the water was drained off. With all of the loose starch removed, we then added water. (I digress for a moment to explain that every Creole kitchen had its own special pot in which nothing but rice was cooked. This was usually a small pot in which no more than 3 cups of raw rice could be prepared.) Now back to the "correct" amount of water: this was a very important step. The wet rice was leveled off in the bottom of the rice pot. Now place the tip of your forefinger *on top* of the raw rice, and carefully and slowly add the water until the water reaches the *first joint* of your forefinger. That's right. If the water was up to the first joint above the rice, you had the right amount. Now a little salt was added to the water and the pot was put on the fire. When it came to a boil, the pot was covered and the heat was lowered until it was barely on. The rice was then cooked for twenty minutes, with no peeking. At this point the pot was uncovered and the rice was fluffed up with a fork (a spoon breaks up the grains). A tablespoon of lard was mixed in with the rice, the cover was replaced, and the rice was allowed to cook for 30 to 40 minutes more. The result was a rice with a marvelous nutlike flavor that was sometimes eaten just as it came from the pot with nothing added. If you've never tasted it this way, I urge you to try it just once.

Now, let's fix one of the old classic Creole dishes, a perfect accompaniment to that Creole rice you've cooked. It's called (what else?) RICE AND CREOLE CHICKEN.

6 Creole or any other ripe tomatoes
2 tbsp. butter
2 tbsp. oil
1 3-lb. frying or broiling chicken, cut in pieces
2 onions, chopped
½ bell pepper, chopped
3 ribs celery, chopped
4 cloves garlic, minced
2 tbsp. flour
¼ tsp. black pepper
¼ tsp. cayenne pepper
1 8-oz. can tomato sauce
2 cups chicken stock
2 thin lemon slices
½ tsp. thyme
2 bay leaves
½ tsp. basil
¼ tsp. powdered cloves
½ tsp. chili powder
salt to taste
6 green onions, chopped
2 tbsp. chopped parsley

*The list of ingredients may look formidable, but this is a comparatively simple dish. First, peel and deseed the tomatoes. Have a pot of boiling water ready. Cut an X into the tomato skin on the opposite end from the stem, drop the tomatoes into the boiling water, leave them there for about 40 seconds, then remove, drain, and allow to cool. Peel the skin off starting at the X cut and you'll find it will slip off easily. Cut each tomato in half and squeeze gently. Out will come some of the seeds. Chop the tomatoes and set them aside.*

*Heat the butter and oil in a heavy pot and over moderate heat brown the chicken pieces. Remove the chicken from the pot, add the onions, bell peppers, celery, and garlic, and sauté over moderate heat for 5 minutes. Sprinkle in the flour, black pepper, and cayenne pepper and cook for 3 minutes more, stirring frequently.*

*Now add the tomatoes, tomato sauce, stock, and everything else except the green onions and parsley. Mix well and then return the chicken to the pot. Bring to a boil, then lower the heat to a simmer and allow to cook, partially covered, for 1 hour, or until the chicken is tender to the touch and the juices are clear. At this point add the green onions and parsley, turn off the heat, cover, and allow to stand 10 minutes before serving over fluffy white rice. Serves four to six.*

# FRIED CHICKEN

Let's look back at a New Orleans institution known, in my younger days, as a "penny party." It would usually start with someone in the group exclaiming, "Let's have a penny party!" (The group consisted of eight to ten enterprising preteenagers in the immediate neighborhood.) Of course, everyone would agree to the suggestion. So the date would be set, usually a Saturday afternoon, and we were ready to start the ball rolling.

The first undertaking was to print the tickets. We had a little printing set we used. It consisted of a small piece of wood with five or six grooves on one side. In the grooves we set the little rubber letters and, with an ink pad, printed our tickets. The whole printing outfit cost a dime at the store. When the tickets were ready, the next task was to walk the neighborhood, knocking at every door, to sell our penny-party invitations. The tickets would be priced at two or three cents, and we would usually wind up with a couple of dollars of starting capital. Now the fun began. With the money we would buy the makings for fudge, pies, and other goodies. We would also buy packaged cakes and candies, which would be sold by the individual piece; and, of course, there were always our parents, who could be counted on for cake donations.

And so the day would finally arrive for the big event. It was always held in someone's backyard. During the week the yard would have been cleaned and made ready for the audience. Now, it was "on with the show." For the price of admission, the patrons were treated to performances by various members of the group. Having a certain propensity for histrionics and a fairly decent ear for music, I would usually sing a couple of songs and recite a poem or two. There were other members of the troupe who might perform simple feats of magic or work up a comedy routine, which was always good for an enthusiastic reaction from the audience. The show-biz part usually lasted an hour or more; some of the players who had finished their performances would double as hawkers of goodies and lemonade. When the curtain closed, the party was over.

There were times when we would net a dollar or two apiece, and so for a time we literally rolled in wealth. Sooner or later, however, the soda fountain, the candy store, and sometimes the pickle barrel would reap the benefits of our newfound wealth. Ah, but as we would philosophize, "easy come, easy go," but now away from the junk food and onto a more nutritious meal that Memere would prepare in her own special way—FRIED CHICKEN, which was just out of this world!

**6 cloves garlic, minced**  
**dash salt**  
**2 eggs, well beaten**  
**2 tbsp. olive oil**  
**1 3-lb. fryer, cut in pieces**  

**½ tsp. of salt**  
**½ tsp. black pepper**  
**¼ tsp. cayenne pepper**  
**1 cup flour**  
**½ cup oil or shortening**  

*In a small dish, mix the garlic with a dash of salt and mash it with a fork. Mix the eggs, garlic, and olive oil. Stir the chicken pieces into the egg mixture and allow the chicken to marinate in the refrigerator for a few hours, turning occasionally. Mix the salt, black pepper, cayenne pepper, and the flour. After the chicken is marinated, remove it from the egg mixture and roll it in the seasoned flour.*

*Heat the oil in a skillet and over a moderate heat fry the chicken until it's golden brown on all sides. Serve with a well-tossed green salad. Serves four.*

# CHICKEN AND RICE CASSEROLE

6 tbsp. butter
2 tbsp. oil
2 medium onions, chopped
1 bell pepper, chopped
½ cup minced green onions
½ pound fresh mushrooms, sliced
½ cup chopped celery
1 tbsp. minced parsley
2 cloves garlic, minced
½ tsp. salt
½ tsp. black pepper
1 tsp. thyme
1 tsp. basil
1 tbsp. Worcestershire sauce
¼ tsp. cayenne pepper
½ tsp. Tabasco
2 cups chicken broth
1 cup sour cream
3 cups cooked, diced chicken
3 cups cooked rice
1 cup toasted almonds

*Heat the butter and oil in a large, heavy skillet. Sauté the onions, bell pepper, green onions, mushrooms, and celery over moderate heat for 5 minutes, stirring frequently. Add the parsley and garlic and simmer for 3 minutes while adding the salt, black pepper, thyme, basil, Worcestershire sauce, cayenne pepper, and Tabasco. Now stir in the broth, mix in well, simmer for 5 minutes, and then slowly add the sour cream. Bring to a simmer and fold in the chicken and rice.*

*Preheat the oven to 375 degrees, pour the mixture into a 2½-quart casserole dish, sprinkle the almonds over the top and bake 30 minutes in the lower part of the oven. Serves six.*

# CHICKEN TETRAZZINI

Before the days of mass-produced vinyl records, Leon was a collector of original phonograph recordings. His first gift to me was a copy of one of his records, Luisa Tetrazzini singing "Una voce poco fa" from *The Barber of Seville*. To accompany the gift, he prepared his own version of Chicken Tetrazzini. Here is the recipe.

**6 tbsp. butter**
**1 lb. fresh mushrooms, sliced**
**4 tbsp. flour**
**1½ cups chicken broth**
**1 cup half-and-half**
**salt and pepper to taste**
**¼ cup sherry**
**3 cups cooked chicken, cut in large dice**
**1 lb. spaghetti, boiled and drained**
**½ cup grated Swiss cheese**
**¼ cup grated Parmesan cheese**
**¼ cup Italian bread crumbs**

*Melt 2 tablespoons of the butter in a heavy saucepan and sauté the mushrooms. Set them aside.*

*Make a cream sauce by melting the remaining 4 tablespoons of butter and adding 4 tablespoons of flour. Over moderate heat stir until the flour and butter are completely mixed, about 2 to 3 minutes, but do not brown. Add the chicken broth, stir until smooth, then add the half-and-half and salt and pepper to taste. Next, add the sherry, mushrooms, and chicken. Mix well in a large bowl, add this mixture to the drained spaghetti, and place in a greased casserole dish. Sprinkle the cheeses and bread crumbs over the top. Bake in a preheated 350-degree oven for 12 to 15 minutes. Serves eight.*

# CHICKEN AMANDINE

1 stick butter
1 tbsp. oil
6 chicken breast halves,
    deboned and skinned
½ tsp. salt
¼ tsp. pepper
4 tbsp. flour

3 oz. slivered almonds
⅓ lb. fresh mushrooms,
    sliced
¼ cup dry sherry
¼ cup chicken stock
½ cup light cream

Melt the butter with the oil in a large skillet. Salt and pepper the chicken breasts and dust them lightly with the flour. Sauté in the butter and oil until the chicken breasts are golden. Remove the chicken and set aside. To the skillet add the almonds and sauté for 5 more minutes over moderate heat stirring constantly. Add the mushrooms; stir gently for a minute or two, then add the sherry and the stock and cook for 2 or 3 minutes more. Mix well. Now slowly add the cream to the liquid and stir.

Place the chicken into a well-greased casserole and pour the mixture over the breasts. Bake in a preheated 325-degree oven for 35 to 45 minutes, or until the chicken is done. Using a sharp fork, pierce the chicken and if the juices are clear or light yellow, it is done; if the juices are pink, cook for 5 minutes more or until the juices are clear or light yellow. Serves four to six.

# DUCK WITH ORANGE SAUCE

"Water, water everywhere
And not a drop [fit] to drink!"

With all of the current furor about the drinking water in our area and the dire consequences of ingesting it, let me share with you the opinion Memere had of "tap" water. Many, many years ago Memere explained that city water was fit only to wash your clothes in! She would explain further that it didn't even do a good job as wash water. If you wanted to live dangerously you might bathe in it, but under no circumstances would you wash your hair in it. Now what has been expressed so far might lead you to ask if we ever took a bath. The answer is "yes"—in rainwater. In our backyard we had an enormous cypress tank and every time it rained all of the rainwater that ran off the roof was diverted into the tank. Since droughts are rare in this area, we very seldom had to resort to the municipal water supply for cooking, bathing, or washing clothes. Of course there were times when the water supply did run low in the cistern and the water became a little sludgy. It was then that the cistern would be decommissioned for a day or so while the inside was cleaned. Then, with the first heavy rain, a good supply of soft cistern water was ensured.

I mentioned that one never used city water for washing one's hair. Cistern water was used for washing hair because it produced lather in abundance (soaps were not as lather-producing in those days). After washing, the hair was roughly rinsed and a weak vinegar solution was rubbed into the scalp. Another rinse with the soft water and the hair was combed and dried, and that was it. Now I'm not saying that this did anything good for the hair, but in their seventies Pepere (my grandfather) and Papete (my father) had luxurious growths of hair that certainly belied their ages.

For the teeth? Well, we never used anything more than a mixture of salt and sodium bicarbonate on our toothbrushes. A lot of today's dentists agree that there is nothing better. Memere would drip the morning coffee with nothing but our backyard water. If the supply ran too low, she would take her pail and borrow a bucket of rainwater from a neighbor. Now I know that some of you may be thinking that cistern water had a marvelous opportunity to develop all sorts of bacteria, but before we get into our recipe, I must remind you that Memere was near her nineties when she left to assume command of that great Creole kitchen in the sky.

Well, so much for water, now how about food? Here's a delightful way to prepare domestic ducks. The light and fragrant orange stuffing and the orange sauce will help to create a festive dish that is sure to please your guests.

*To prepare the sauce:*

**1 cup orange marmalade**
**½ cup freshly squeezed orange juice**

**¼ cup freshly grated orange peel**
**2 tbsp. orange liqueur**

*Combine these ingredients in a saucepan and cook over very low heat until the sauce is smooth. Set the sauce aside, but keep it warm.*

*To prepare the ducks:*

**2 4- to 5-lb. domestic ducks (can be frozen)**
**1 tsp. salt**

**½ tsp. black pepper**
**½ tsp. cayenne pepper**
**1 tsp. paprika**

*Make four batches of the salt, pepper, and paprika mixture. Mix each batch separately.*

*Wash the ducks and dry the insides very well. Remove the fat, as much as possible. Rub the inside of each duck with a batch of the salt, black and cayenne pepper and paprika mixture. Place the following stuffing inside each duck:*

**1 orange, thinly sliced**
**1 onion, thinly sliced**

**2 cloves garlic, minced**

*Gently prick the skin here and there, especially on the breasts and thighs. Now rub the outside of the ducks with the salt-pepper-paprika mixture.*

*To prepare the roasting pan:*

**1 stalk celery, finely chopped**
**1 bunch green onions, finely chopped**
**1 medium white onion, finely chopped**
**2 cloves garlic, minced**
**1 small bell pepper, finely chopped**
**1 cup water**
**1 cup white wine**

*Mix the above vegetables together; set the ducks on top the vegetables. Gently add the water and the wine.*

*In a preheated 450-degree oven, bake the ducks for 25 minutes; turn the ducks breast side down, reduce the heat to 350 degrees, and bake about 30 minutes. Turn the ducks breast side up and continue baking for an additional 1 hour and 25 minutes. Baste the ducks every half hour with juices from the baking pan. The ducks are done when they are tender to the touch, the drumsticks move easily in their sockets, and the juice is clear when the drumsticks are pierced with a fork.*

*At this point remove the ducks to a heatproof platter. Stick the skin again in several places with your fork. Brush the ducks with the warm orange sauce and roast in a preheated 425-degree oven for 5 minutes or until the skin is brown and crisp. Baste the duck with the sauce once or twice. Serves eight.*

# WILD DUCK WITH SWEET POTATOES

6 wild ducks
salt and pepper to taste
Tabasco
2 sweet potatoes
2 apples, peeled and diced

3 medium onions, chopped
½ stick butter
1½ cups burgundy
½ lb. mushrooms, sliced

*The ducks should be cleaned and dressed, then washed and wiped dry. Now season the ducks inside and out with the salt, pepper, and a few drops of Tabasco.*

*Boil the sweet potatoes until they are partially cooked (about 5 minutes), then peel and dice them. Mix together the sweet potatoes, apples, and onions and then loosely stuff the ducks with the mixture. Put the ducks in a heavy baking pan with a tight lid and bake in a 350-degree oven for 2 hours. As soon as the ducks are in the oven, melt the butter and mix it with the wine. While the ducks are baking, baste them with the butter and wine mixture about every 15 minutes.*

*When the ducks are tender (when the drumsticks move freely in the socket), remove the cover and add the mushrooms to the baking pan. Allow the ducks to brown in the oven while you baste them frequently. Serve with crisp French bread and a bottle of hearty Burgundy. Serves six.*

# QUAIL IN WINE SAUCE

8 fine, fat quail
1 lemon
salt
black pepper
3 tbsp. oil
6 tbsp. butter
⅓ cup finely chopped green
  onions
1 white onion, finely
  chopped
1 cup finely chopped
  mushrooms
1 tbsp. finely chopped fresh
  parsley
1½ cups white wine

*Wash and dry the quail. Rub the inside and outside of each quail with the cut side of half a lemon (you will use both halves). Season the quail inside and out with salt and pepper. Tie the drumsticks of each quail together with kitchen twine. Place the oil and 3 tablespoons of butter in a heavy Dutch oven and melt over moderate heat. Put in the quail, two at a time, and sauté over moderate heat until all sides are golden brown (about 5 to 10 minutes per quail). Remove the quail and set them aside.*

*Drain all the oil from the Dutch oven and put in the remaining 3 tablespoons of butter; add the green onions and white onion when the butter foams and, over moderate heat, stirring constantly, cook until the onions are soft. Add the mushrooms and parsley and cook for 3 or 4 minutes, then add the wine. Stir until all vegetables are well blended. Now return the birds to the pot. Reduce the heat to a simmer and cook, covered, for 30 minutes, basting frequently and adding a little water. The birds will burn if the liquid evaporates, so maintain about an inch of sauce in the pot. Serve with brown or wild rice. Serves four.*

# ROAST GOOSE

One Christmas we decided to pattern our family dinner after the meal eaten by the Cratchit family of Tiny Tim. So we looked up Charles Dickens's description. I still remember two items on the menu—Roast Goose and Plum Pudding—and there were lots of other tasty morsels. We had fun!

Here's how to prepare the goose. Probably the only kind of goose you will find will be frozen. The one we cooked weighed about 9 pounds. You don't want one larger than 11 pounds because it may be too tough. Place the frozen goose in a pan in the refrigerator a day or two ahead of time so it can defrost.

| | |
|---|---|
| 1 9- to 10-lb. goose | ⅔ cup dry white wine |
| salt and pepper | ½ tsp. nutmeg |
| Fruit and Nut Stuffing | 2 tbsp. butter (room |
| (recipe follows) | temperature) |
| ½ cup apricot jam or | |
| preserves | |

*Pull out all of the loose fat from the cavity of the goose as well as around the neck. Rinse the goose and pat dry. Rub inside and out with salt and pepper. Prick the skin all over the thighs, the back, and breast. (This is necessary to release the fat as the bird roasts.) Fill loosely with the stuffing and sew or skewer the openings. Place the goose breast-side up on a rack in an uncovered roasting pan and roast in a 325-degree oven for about 20 to 25 minutes per pound. A goose has a heavy layer of fat just beneath the skin, so as this renders out remove the fat from the roasting pan with a bulb baster.*

*Combine the jam, wine, nutmeg, and butter to make the basting sauce. Set aside.*

*The stuffed goose should be done in about 3 hours—when the drumsticks move slightly in their sockets and when the juices are yellow as you pierce a fleshy part with a fork. Baste the goose with the sauce and let the goose rest for about 20 minutes before carving on the serving platter.*

Pour out all of the fat from the pan but leave the brown roasting juices. Pour in the sauce and on a low heat simmer while you scrape up the juices from the pan. When the liquid has reduced by about one-fourth, add 2 tbsp. warm butter and whisk to mix thoroughly. Serve with the roast goose. Serves six to eight.

# FRUIT AND NUT STUFFING

3 tart apples, peeled and
   diced
2 tbsp. lemon juice
¼ cup butter
¼ cup chopped onion
1 cup chopped celery leaves
   and stalks
2 tbsp. minced fresh parsley

1 cup stale French bread
   cubes
1 cup chopped pecans
¼ cup white wine
¼ tsp. nutmeg
¼ cup brown sugar
salt and pepper to taste

*Sprinkle the apples with lemon juice.*

*Heat the butter in a large skillet. Add the onion, celery and parsley and cook until the onions are soft.*

*Add the bread, pecans, wine, nutmeg, and sugar. Cook over low heat, stirring constantly, about 3 minutes; be sure everything is well mixed. Salt and pepper to taste.*

# TURKEY POULETTE

8 slices bread, toasted and
  buttered
enough sliced turkey meat
  to cover 8 slices of bread
6 slices crispy bacon,
  crumbled
5 tbsp. butter
6 green onions, finely
  chopped
4 tbsp. flour

3 cups milk
1 cup grated cheddar
  cheese
¼ cup grated Parmesan
  cheese
salt and black pepper to
  taste
1 dash Tabasco
½ tsp. paprika

*Toast the bread, butter it, and place 2 slices each on 4 plates. Spread the sliced turkey over the bread and sprinkle the crumbled bacon over the turkey.*

*For the sauce, melt the butter in a skillet and sauté the green onions for 5 minutes. Over low heat, add the flour, stir, and cook for 3 more minutes. Continue to stir as you add the milk slowly and bring the mixture to a simmer. As the sauce thickens add ½ cup of the cheddar cheese, all the Parmesan, and salt, pepper, and Tabasco to taste. Simmer until the cheese melts, then distribute the sauce over the turkey and bacon. Spread the rest of the cheese on top, sprinkle the paprika over the sauce and broil just until the cheese melts. Serves four.*

# egg dishes

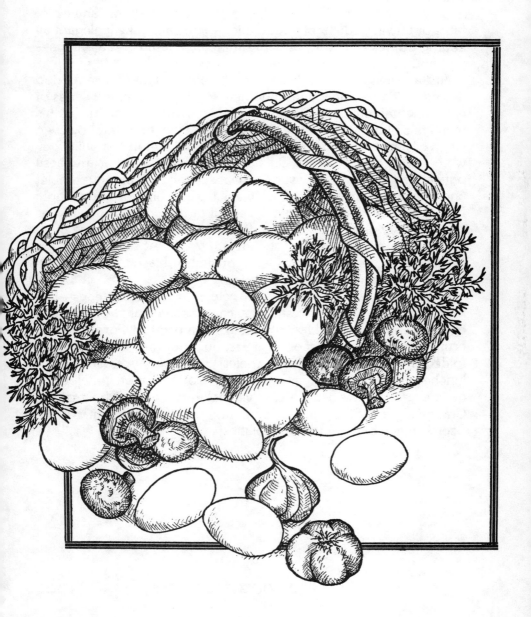

In the hands of a capable cook eggs are like the pigments that a painter uses to create a work of art. The pigments may be nothing but dabs of color, but the artist will bring them together to become a whole picture.

So it is with eggs. They can be combined with almost any vegetable or any ingredient of your choice—you can make it elegant by adding truffles or caviar, or very simple by adding green onions—and you will have created a work of art.

Just as Picasso had his Blue Period, Leon had his Omelet Period during which he applied his ingenuity to the creation of a series of experimental omelets. To ensure objective criticism he let his teenage children taste these specialties. He went too far, however, when he served the omelets to them early in the morning while they were still in bed. Now an Omelet aux Fines Herbes or a cheese omelet was just dandy, but soon he was serving an asparagus omelet and then a tomato omelet. Each week it was a bit more exotic until finally a Grand Marnier omelet, served at the crack of dawn, was unanimously given the thumbs-down verdict. It would have been relished at midnight or 1 A.M., but not 7 A.M. At this point Leon decided that his guinea pigs were obviously biased and had "no taste"; thus ended his Omelet Period.

There is an almost unlimited variety of ways to use eggs—just make sure they are very fresh. They can be served at any meal. The egg may appear at breakfast poached or as an omelet. For an elegant brunch try Eggs Benedict or Eggs Sardou. They may have crabmeat folded into them (Crabmeat Omelet) or they may be served for luncheon as Creamed Eggs on Toast. A Potato-Onion Omelet or a quiche are other possibilities. I've included two quiche recipes: Crabmeat and Spinach. For something a little different try the Scotch Eggs. Explore the possibilities!

# EGGS BENEDICT

2 English muffins, split and
  toasted
4 thin slices fried ham
4 poached eggs

1 cup Hollandaise Sauce
  (see index)
paprika

*Place the English muffins on two plates. Cover with ham, eggs, and one-fourth of the hollandaise sauce over each egg. Sprinkle with paprika. Serve immediately. Serves two.*

# EGGS SARDOU

2 cups Creamed Spinach
  (see index)
1 14-oz. can artichoke
  bottoms
2 cups water

½ tsp. salt
8 poached eggs
2 cups Hollandaise Sauce
  (see index)

*Make the creamed spinach but do not add the Parmesan cheese and crumbs. Set aside.*

*Heat the water and add salt. When water is at a simmer, add the artichoke bottoms and simmer for 2 minutes. Remove from water, drain on paper towels, and keep warm. Poach eggs. Prepare Hollandaise Sauce.*

*Divide the spinach into four equal portions. Place two artichoke bottoms on a warm serving plate and fill with spinach; cover each with a poached egg. Ladle the Hollandaise Sauce over the eggs. Repeat for other servings. Serve immediately. Serves four.*

# CREAMED EGGS ON TOAST

Memere really had a way with eggs! And I'll never forget the creamy, tender omelets that she would fix for breakfast! Her omelet pan, which hung on the kitchen wall, was used *only* for omelets. The pan would be heated until it was very hot. Sweet butter was melted in the pan, and at just the right moment a gentle swoosh could be heard as she added the lightly beaten eggs. In less than a minute a moist, golden omelet was on the plate, brushed with a little melted butter, ready to be eaten.

Everyone in the family enjoyed eggs, and so we used a lot of them. To keep a good supply of fresh eggs always in the kitchen, Memere always had a yard full of chickens. Our chickens were always the larger, heavier breeds—Barred Rocks or Rhode Island Reds. Some yards in the neighborhood were populated with White Leghorn hens, which were the best layers, no argument there, but Memere always felt that since we also ate a lot of chicken, the heavier chickens—even though they laid fewer eggs—were a good compromise. Besides, the Leghorns would very seldom set, whereas the large, heavy hens were always wanting to raise a brood of chicks.

It was usually in the spring or early summer when some of the hens would take a notion to set. You could tell by watching those hens that were always sitting on the nest. Now we always kept a couple of roosters in the yard so that the eggs we collected would be fertile. When one of the hens gave any indication that she wanted to set, Memere would watch her carefully. Sometimes she would even go into the chicken house and deliberately run the hen out into the yard. She would do this two or three times, and if the hen persisted we knew it was no false alarm. Now the hen was transferred to another nest and 18 to 24 eggs were placed under her. (The number always depended upon the size of the hen.) How marvelous it was to watch a little beak appear through the egg shell and crack the shell enough for the little chick to free itself! Soon there was a brood of twenty or so little chicks. When the chicks were strong enough, the hen was put in the yard under a cage made of slats, which allowed the chicks to run around the yard but kept the mother in the cage. If the other chickens bothered the little ones, they would run between the slats to safety near the mother hen.

So we always had a good supply of eggs on hand, and often for a Sunday-night supper Memere would fix her CREAMED EGGS ON TOAST.

6 tbsp. sweet butter
1 medium onion, finely chopped
4 green onions, finely chopped
3 tbsp. flour

6 hard-cooked eggs, sliced medium-thick
1 cup heavy cream
1 tsp. celery seed
½ tsp. cayenne pepper
6 slices buttered toast

*Melt the butter in a saucepan. Add the onion and green onions, and simmer over low heat for 10 minutes, stirring constantly. Sprinkle in the flour, mix well, and cook over very low heat for 4 minutes. Cut the eggs into the sauce and mix gently. Let this mixture simmer for 2 minutes; while it's simmering add the cream and seasonings. Arrange a slice of toast on each plate and distribute the sauce and eggs over the toast. Serves three to six.*

# SCOTCH EGGS

1 lb. pork sausage
¼ tsp. thyme
¼ tsp. sage
¼ tsp. poultry seasoning
1 tbsp. minced parsley
8 hard-cooked eggs
½ cup flour plus 1 cup

¼ tsp. salt
½ tsp. black pepper
¼ tsp. cayenne pepper
2 eggs, lightly beaten
½ cup bread crumbs
3 cups peanut oil

Combine the sausage, thyme, sage, poultry seasoning, and parsley in a large bowl. Blend well and divide into 8 equal portions.

Dust the peeled eggs with the ½ cup of flour.

Flatten each portion of the sausage mixture and put an egg in the center. Bring the sausage mixture up around the sides of the egg so that the egg is completely covered with the sausage mixture.

Mix the remaining flour with the salt and peppers. Roll the sausage-covered eggs in this seasoned flour, then in the beaten eggs, and finally in the bread crumbs.

Deep-fry the covered eggs in peanut oil for 10 minutes, until the sausage is thoroughly cooked. Serve hot or cold. This makes a delicious breakfast; the eggs can also be cut in thick segments and used as a tasty appetizer.

# HOW TO POACH AN EGG

4 cups water
2 tsp. vinegar
2 eggs

2 slices buttered toast or 1
split and toasted English
muffin

Heat water in a skillet or saucepan to a simmer. Add the vinegar. Heat back to a simmer.

Break one egg into a saucer.

Stir the simmering water with a spoon to make it swirl. Tilt the saucer closely over the water and let the egg slip from the saucer into the middle of the swirling water. Keep the water at a simmer and proceed with the second egg in the same manner.

Baste the eggs by spooning hot water over the eggs. Cook for four minutes or until the whites are set; the yolks should remain soft. Remove from the water with a slotted spoon.

Place on toast or English muffin and serve with the sauce of your choice.

Note: If you wish to have a brunch and serve Eggs Benedict or Eggs Sardou, the eggs may be poached and placed in a deep bowl of cold water and refrigerated. When ready to serve, remove one egg at a time with a slotted spoon and place in hot salted water for about 1 minute to reheat.

# OMELETS

Every now and then the world of cooking seems to produce a plethora of articles about omelets. You are usually made to feel that you need a doctorate from the Cordon Bleu, plus the skill of a culinary virtuoso, to produce a good omelet. Well, pish tush dear friend, that just isn't so! Take Memere and Mamete. They were great omelet makers. They did it simply, without fanfare, without so much as a blow on the pan handle or contortionistic egg flipping. And yet what a sight their golden, fluffy omelets were—the melt-in-your-mouth kind! And so I figured, to remove the myth, mystique, and magic from omelet-making, I'll let you in on how Memere went about her omelet creation.

The first necessity is a good omelet pan. This is an absolute essential! What's more, the pan, once seasoned, should forevermore be used for nothing but omelets. The pan should be as thick as possible. Why thick? Well, when the pan is heated to the proper heat, the eggs are poured in. Now if the pan is a thin one, it cools off too much to cook the omelet properly. So get a thick one. Memere's was a cast-iron skillet with sloping sides, not the straight-sided kind. The one I use is a cast-aluminum pan, almost half an inch thick. It's been in use about twenty years and has been washed once, the day I got it! So get a good thick pan, wash it, scour it, and then season it. You can forget about washing it for as long as you use it. Wipe it with a paper towel after use.

But let's get back to a few simple rules that, if you'll follow them, will have you turning out omelets which could easily incur the envy of Mère Poularde. (She was supposed to have invented the omelet, although I'm sure the Chinese were cooking omelets long before her time.) As I've said, an omelet has to be quickly cooked in a very hot pan. This means that from the time the eggs are poured into the pan to the completed omelet should take less than a minute. If they cook more than a minute, the eggs will be overcooked. Okay, let's assemble everything and cook the omelet.

Take 3 eggs from the refrigerator and allow about 2 hours for them to reach room temperature (this step is necessary to ensure a properly cooked omelet). You'll need a bowl in which to break the eggs, a fork to stir the eggs as they cook, seasoning, some butter, and a plate for the finished product. Before we start, I must point out that an omelet is not scrambled eggs; these are something altogether different. So we now break the eggs into the bowl, then place the pan over high heat. While the pan is heating, we add 2 tablespoons of water to the eggs (no milk or cream), a little salt, and, if possible, some freshly ground black pepper. Now we wait until the pan is very hot. You can usually tell by feeling the handle close to the pan. When the handle becomes very hot to the touch, the pan is ready. Butter goes into the pan and the pan is moved about and tilted as the butter melts, so as to spread it over the bottom and sides. The butter will froth up and then subside; at this point it will start to darken in color. We are now ready for the eggs—and you must act quickly now so the butter will not burn. Beat the eggs with the fork, no more than 30 times, and then pour them into the pan. If you hear a gentle "whoosh," your pan is hot enough.

Now comes the formation of the omelet. Allow the eggs to set for about 6 seconds and then take the fork and pull the edges into the center. What you are trying to do is keep the egg that is cooked from cooking any longer and to allow the liquid part to flow into the bottom of the pan. This process should take about 30 seconds. Then the omelet is ready; the center should still be semi-liquid. Now comes a little tricky part. With your fork, fold over just a little of the left edge of the omelet. (Once you try it, you'll find it easy to do.) With the plate in your right hand and the pan in your left, bring the pan and the plate together and roll the omelet out onto the plate. This is a quick movement and requires almost turning the pan upside down with the left hand. As the pan is turned, the omelet rolls out and into a cigar shape. Now brush a little melted butter over it and voilà: a beautiful golden, fluffy omelet. But I did tell you we were going to watch Memere do it, didn't I? Well, trust me, I've told you just exactly how she turned out those omelet treats.

The omelet can be served as simple as the recipe just given or can be made with a variety of fillings.

**3 eggs**
**2 tbsp. water**
**dash of salt**

**¼ tsp. freshly ground black**
**pepper**
**2 tbsp. butter**

# CRABMEAT OMELET

3 eggs
3 tsp. cold water
2 drops Tabasco
salt and pepper to taste

2 tbsp. melted butter
⅓ cup lump crabmeat
parsley (garnish)

*Break the eggs into a mixing bowl; add the water, Tabasco, salt, and pepper. Melt the butter in an omelet pan. (Do not allow it to burn.) Beat the eggs 30 strokes with a fork. Pour the eggs into the melted butter. Stir the eggs with a fork, working the cooked egg to the center of the pan. Add the crabmeat to the top of the omelet after cooking 1½ minutes. (The total cooking time of this omelet is 2 minutes.) Fold the omelet over carefully onto a warm plate. Garnish with parsley. Serves one as a main dish.*

# POTATO-ONION SUPPER OMELET

6 tbsp. vegetable oil
2 potatoes, peeled and cut
   into ⅜-inch wide strips
2 tbsp. butter
1 onion, coarsely chopped

5 eggs, lightly beaten
salt
black pepper
Tabasco
parsley (garnish)

*Heat the oil in a large skillet. Add the potatoes and fry them until they are tender, golden brown, and crisp, about 6 to 8 minutes. Remove the potatoes and drain them on paper towels. Pour off all but 2 tablespoons of the oil. Add the butter; when it foams, add the onions and sauté over low heat until the onions are soft. Put the potatoes back in the skillet. When they are warm, add the beaten eggs, salt, pepper, and Tabasco. Stir the mixture only until the ingredients are well combined, then allow to cook undisturbed over low heat until the eggs have cooked for about 1 minute. This omelet is not folded. Serve immediately on warm plates, garnished with fresh parsley. Serves two.*

*Note: Hot French bread goes well with this for a Sunday night supper.*

# CRABMEAT QUICHE

**1 10-inch unbaked pie crust**
**(see index)**

**1 egg, lightly beaten**

*Prick the unbaked pie crust on the bottom with a fork and brush with the beaten egg. (If your pie crust has cracks in it, or has been broken, mend the shell by moistening the edges with a little water and press the edges together.) Bake in the middle of a preheated 400-degree oven for 8 or 9 minutes. Remove the pie crust and cool.*

*Reduce the oven temperature to 375 degrees.*

*To prepare the filling:*

**1 cup crabmeat**
**2 tbsp. finely chopped green**
**  onions**
**1 tbsp. minced fresh parsley**
**2 tbsp. butter**
**1 tbsp. flour**
**1½ tbsp. dry white wine**

**3 large eggs**
**1⅓ cup heavy cream**
**1 tsp. salt**
**⅛ tsp. cayenne pepper**
**¼ tsp. white pepper**
**⅓ cup grated Swiss cheese**

*Remove any pieces of shell from the crabmeat. Spoon it into the pie crust.*

*Sauté the green onions and the parsley in the butter for one minute over moderate heat. Do not brown. Reduce the heat to low, add the flour and stir constantly for one minute. Add the wine and cook for another minute, stirring constantly. Remove from the heat. Set aside.*

*Combine the eggs, cream, salt, cayenne and white peppers, and cheese. Mix thoroughly and then add the green onion and parsley mixture. Mix well, and gently pour all of this over the crabmeat in the pie crust.*

*Bake in a 375-degree oven for 35 to 40 minutes or until the quiche is firmly set in the center. Serves four to six.*

# SPINACH QUICHE

**1 unbaked pastry shell to fit a 10-inch quiche pan**

**1 egg, slightly beaten**

*Prick the unbaked pie crust on the bottom with a fork and brush with the beaten egg. (If your pastry shell has cracks in it, or has been broken, mend the shell by moistening the edges with a little water and press the edges together.) Bake in the middle of a preheated 400-degree oven for 8 or 9 minutes. Remove the pie crust and cool.*

*Reduce oven temperature to 375 degrees.*

*To prepare the filling:*

**⅓ cup finely chopped green onions**
**3 tbsp. finely chopped fresh parsley**
**2 tbsp. butter**
**1 cup cooked spinach, chopped and drained**
**½ tsp. salt**
**⅛ tsp. cayenne pepper**

**¼ tsp. black pepper**
**¼ tsp. grated nutmeg**
**1 tbsp. Worcestershire Sauce**
**3 large eggs, slightly beaten**
**⅓ cup grated Swiss cheese**
**3 tbsp. grated Parmesan cheese**
**1⅓ cups heavy cream**

*Sauté the green onions and parsley in the butter for 1 minute over moderate heat. Do not brown. Reduce the heat; add the spinach, salt, peppers, nutmeg and Worcestershire sauce. Mix well, then remove from the heat.*

*Combine the eggs, cheese, and cream. Add to the spinach mixture and pour into the partially baked pie crust.*

*Bake in a 375-degree oven for 35 to 40 minutes or until the quiche is firmly set in the center and is golden brown. Serves four to six.*

*vegetables*

We in New Orleans live in an area blessed with a mild climate and a lot of sunshine and rain, so we have an abundant supply of fresh vegetables available almost year round. Indeed, many of our home gardens today include a "vegetable patch." Nestled between the Creole tomato plants and the bell peppers, you'll find marigolds blooming merrily (the marigolds help to repel the insects). Green onions and parsley are often snipped from our own garden beds. For many who have the time, their pantries display jars of home-grown beans, pickled okra, and pickles from their cucumber crop. Our fences are covered with mirlitons (known as chayotes in many places). Beans and eggplant bushes flourish in our hot and humid summer days.

Whether you grow your own vegetables or buy fresh vegetables at the supermarket, you can enjoy down-home-style Creole vegetables. In this section I have included recipes for Eleanor's Lima Beans with Pickled Pork, and Mary Lou's Green Beans. The lima beans are traditionally cooked on a low simmer for 4 to 6 hours and are unbelievably good.

Another Creole favorite is the stuffed vegetable. Eggplants, green peppers, tomatoes, cabbage, mirlitons, mushrooms, and artichokes are all excellent for stuffing. Creole cooks transform the lowliest vegetable into fancy fare by scooping out their pulp and stuffing the shells with ham, meat, seafood, or a savory rice mixture. Ed's Mirliton Stuffed with Crawfish is an excellent example of the way in which a simple vegetable can become an elegant dish.

Creole cooks are also very fond of artichokes. Sometimes we simply boil artichokes in salted water and serve them with a sauce. For more formal occasions, Leon's Stuffed Artichokes will be well received.

The list of Creole vegetables is endless—included in this section are some of our favorites.

# HOW TO BOIL ARTICHOKES

Remove the artichoke stem at the base with a knife so that the artichoke will stand upright. Break off the small leaves at the base; slice ¾ of an inch off the top of the artichoke and trim off the points of the rest of the leaves with scissors. Wash under cold water.

Place the artichokes in a large container of cold water, with 1 tablespoon of vinegar per quart of water. This prevents the artichokes from discoloring. Place a soup plate on top of the artichokes to keep them submerged. Let stand for 1 hour.

Artichokes must be boiled in a large quantity of water. Fill a large stainless steel pot (iron or aluminum will turn artichokes a gray color) with water and add 1½ teaspoons salt per quart of water. When the water comes to a rolling boil, add the artichokes. When the water comes back to a boil, reduce the heat slightly, partially cover the pot and cook on a low boil for 45 minutes to 1 hour. The artichokes are done when the leaves pull out easily and the bottoms are fork tender.

Boiled artichokes are delicious when served as an appetizer or in place of a salad. Try DAVID'S SAUCE FOR ARTICHOKES (recipe follows).

# DAVID'S SAUCE FOR ARTICHOKES

3 tbsp. mayonnaise
1 tbsp. yellow mustard or 1 tsp. Colman's dried mustard
2 tbsp. Italian bread crumbs
2 tsp. cider vinegar
1 tbsp. Worcestershire sauce

Mix all the ingredients together. Dip the cooked artichoke leaves in this sauce for a tasty treat.

# LEON'S STUFFED ARTICHOKES

4 medium artichokes
cold water (enough to cover artichokes)
1 tbsp. lemon juice
2 cups seasoned bread crumbs
8 to 10 cloves garlic, minced
½ cup minced green onions

2 tbsp. minced fresh parsley
⅔ cup grated Parmesan cheese
salt and pepper to taste
10 drops Tabasco
1 egg, slightly beaten
⅔ cup olive oil (more may be necessary) plus 3 tbsp. for each artichoke

Trim the stem of the artichokes so they will stand upright. Strip off the coarse outer leaves. With a sharp knife, cut about ½ inch from the top and with a pair of scissors trim the ends off each leaf. Throw into cold water to wash well, adding the lemon juice.

In a large bowl mix all the remaining ingredients except the egg and olive oil. Now add the slightly beaten egg and ⅓ cup of the olive oil. (Use your hands to mix this.) Work the ingredients until thoroughly blended and slightly moistened (more olive oil may be necessary). Spread the leaves of each artichoke and fill with the stuffing.

Place the artichokes in a deep pot that has a tight fitting lid. Put about ½ inch of water in the pot; cover and steam on low heat for 1 hour. After 30 minutes check to see if more water is necessary. When a leaf can be removed easily, the artichokes are cooked. Remove the lid. Dribble 3 tablespoons of olive oil over each artichoke making sure that a little oil has penetrated in between each leaf. Replace the lid and allow them to cool in the covered pot. Serves four.

# ELEANOR'S LIMA BEANS WITH PICKLED PORK

3 cups lima beans
1 lb. pickled pork or slab
  bacon
1 16-oz. can tomatoes
water (enough to cover
  beans by 2 inches)
1 large onion, coarsely
  chopped
¼ tsp. powdered allspice
½ tsp. basil

½ tsp. dried thyme
½ tsp. black pepper
¼ tsp. cayenne pepper
dash Tabasco
2 bay leaves
salt
½ cup coarsely chopped
  green onions
cooked rice

*Wash the beans, put them in a large pot, cover them with water, and soak overnight. The next day, drain and place in a large pot with the pickled pork, tomatoes, and enough water to cover the beans by 2 inches. Add the onion, allspice, basil, thyme, black and cayenne pepper, Tabasco, and bay leaves. Bring to a boil and turn the heat to low. Stir frequently and add more water as necessary. Cook for 2 hours or until the beans are tender. Add salt and green onion. Serve over hot rice. Serves six.*

*Note: Pickled pork is a fatty pork shoulder marinated in brine. We purchase it packaged in our supermarkets and use it to season our beans and gumbos.*

# MARY LOU'S GREEN BEANS

2 lbs. fresh green beans
½ lb. sweet pickled pork,
  cut into ½-inch pieces
1 tbsp. oil
1 tbsp. butter
2 medium onions, finely
  chopped
2 cloves garlic, minced
½ tsp. sugar

3½ cups water
1 tsp. black pepper
½ tsp. thyme
1 tsp. sweet basil
2 dashes Tabasco
1 tsp. white vinegar
1 lb. potatoes, peeled and
  quartered
salt to taste

Snip the ends from the beans and break the beans into 2-inch pieces. Rinse them in cold water. Drain and set aside.

In a heavy-bottomed Dutch oven, brown the meat in the oil and butter over moderate heat. Then, remove the pork from the pot, and add the onions. Over low heat sauté the onions very slowly, stirring constantly until they're soft and golden brown; add the garlic and continue stirring until the aroma of the garlic is released. Now add the sugar and stir constantly until the sugar caramelizes, then add the water and the seasonings. Return the meat to the pot, bring the liquid to a boil, then reduce the heat to a simmer, cover the pot, and cook for 30 minutes, stirring occasionally.

Add the potatoes and the beans to the pot. Bring liquid up to boil again; reduce to a low simmer and cover the pot. Cook on low simmer for 30 minutes or until the potatoes are fork tender. The pickled pork has made the mixture salty so you may not need to add salt, but check to adjust seasonings.

This is an example of our good one-pot soul-food dishes. As a main meal we have this with French bread or corn bread for a most satisfying meal. Serves six to eight.

# KELLY'S TANGY BEETS

**1 bunch fresh beets or 2
8-oz. cans small beets**
**2 tbsp. cornstarch**
**2 tbsp. water**

**1 cup orange juice**
**¼ cup sugar**
**dash salt**
**1 tbsp. butter**

*If you are using fresh beets, cut off the beet tops leaving 1 inch of the tops to prevent bleeding.*

*Wash the beets. Place in boiling salted water, using enough water to cover the whole beets by 2 inches. Cover and boil until tender. Depending upon the size of the beets, the cooking time will vary from 20 to 60 minutes for young beets and from 1 to 2 hours for mature beets. When the beets are tender, remove from the pot. When they are cool, peel and slice them into ¼-inch thick pieces. Set aside.*

*If you are using canned beets, drain and proceed as follows.*

*Mix the cornstarch and water together. Combine the mixture with the orange juice, sugar, salt, and butter in the top of a double boiler. Cook until the sauce has thickened (about 5 minutes). Place the beets in the sauce and mix until the beets are warm. Serve immediately. Serves four to six.*

*Note: This is a tasty accompaniment to Crown Roast of Pork (see index) or Kidneys Bordelaise (see index).*

# CABBAGE AU GRATIN

1 2½- to 3-lb. head fresh
  cabbage
3 qts. water
1 tsp. salt
½ cup grated American
  cheese

1 cup medium White Sauce
  (see index)
½ cup bread crumbs
paprika

*Remove any damaged outer leaves from the cabbage. Separate the leaves. In a large pot bring the water and salt to a rapid boil. Add the cabbage leaves and boil for 10 minutes, then drain.*

*Add the grated cheese to the prepared White Sauce.*

*Arrange the cabbage in a layer in a greased casserole, ladle the sauce over it, place another layer of cabbage leaves, and then ladle on more sauce. Repeat. On top of the last layer of sauce lightly sprinkle the bread crumbs and paprika.*

*Bake in a preheated 350-degree oven for 20 to 25 minutes or until golden brown. Serves six to eight.*

# STUFFED CABBAGE ROLLS

1 medium head cabbage
½ stick butter
1 onion, chopped
4 green onions, chopped
4 cloves garlic, chopped
2 stalks celery, chopped
½ green pepper, chopped
1 cup finely chopped boiled
  ham
½ cup beef stock

½ tsp. powdered thyme
5 drops Tabasco
½ tsp. chili powder
salt and pepper to taste
1½ cups cooked rice
1 32-oz. jar sauerkraut,
  drained
1 8-oz. can tomato sauce
¼ cup grated Parmesan
  cheese

Boil the whole cabbage in a large pot until the leaves are tender, about 10 minutes. Remove it from the water, drain, and allow it to cool. Meanwhile, melt the butter and sauté the onion, green onions, garlic, celery, green pepper, and ham over low heat. Cook for 5 minutes, stirring constantly, and then add the stock. Raise the heat and bring the liquid to a boil. While it is boiling, add the thyme, Tabasco, chili powder, and salt and pepper. Cook until almost all the liquid is gone; then remove from the heat and stir in the rice. Set the stuffing aside.

Prepare the cabbage leaves. Very carefully remove the leaves by cutting them loose from the center and peeling them off.

Spread the sauerkraut over the bottom of a large baking dish. Now put a heaping tablespoon of the stuffing in the center of each cabbage leaf, fold in the sides of the leaf, and roll the leaf tightly. Place the rolled leaf with the loose end down in the bed of sauerkraut. Stuff as many leaves as it takes to cover the kraut with the rolls. Make casserole one layer deep. Now spoon the tomato sauce over each roll, then sprinkle the Parmesan cheese over the sauce. Preheat the oven to 375 degrees and place the pan in the oven for 45 minutes. This can be a side dish or an entrée. Serves six to eight.

# BLANCHE'S STEWED CORN

In the summer when the new corn crop was ready, the Creole housewife served it not only boiled and buttered on the cob, but also in various other ways. Here's a Soniat family favorite from Leon's sister Blanche.

**8 ears fresh white corn**
**3 tbsp. vegetable oil**
**3 tbsp. flour**
**1 large onion, finely chopped**
**2 8-oz. cans tomato sauce**
**3 cups water**
**4 cloves garlic, minced**
**3 bay leaves**
**½ tsp. thyme**

**¼ tsp. allspice**
**¼ tsp. black pepper**
**¼ tsp. white pepper**
**¼ tsp. cayenne pepper**
**dash Tabasco**
**1 lb. raw ham, cut in ½-inch cubes**
**¼ cup minced fresh parsley**
**cooked rice**

*Remove the husks and silk from the corn. Standing an ear of corn on one end, use a sharp knife and cut the kernels close to the cob. Now, using a spoon or the dull side of the knife, scrape the cob to remove all the pulp. Place all the cut corn in a bowl, cover, and set aside until ready to use.*

*Place the oil in a heavy Dutch oven; add the flour and stir constantly for 3 or 4 minutes over moderate heat until the roux is a nut-brown color. Add the onion, lower the heat, and simmer until the onion is soft. Next add the tomato sauce. Stir constantly as it simmers. When the sauce is reduced by two-thirds, add the water. Raise the heat and let the water come to a low boil. Then add the garlic, bay leaves, thyme, allspice, black pepper, white pepper, cayenne pepper, and Tabasco. Reduce the heat and cover. Simmer for about one hour, stirring occasionally. Then add the ham, bring the liquid in the pot back to a gentle boil, then lower to simmer, cover, and cook for an additional hour. Now add the corn, and, stirring occasionally, simmer 15 to 20 minutes. Add the fresh parsley and serve over hot, fluffy rice. Serves eight to twelve.*

# AUBERGINE TOMATES

You could bet that winter had ended and the cold weather was over when Memere began to move her tomato plants. They had enjoyed the warmth of the kitchen for a few weeks and now it was time to be replanted outside. There were other signs, too. There was the fertilizing of the pecan tree. Memere's way was to wait until just before the ends of the pecan boughs began to sprout their little leaves and then pour the fertilizer into little holes we had dug around the tree. I learned that any nourishment, to be effective, had to be placed as far from the tree as the branches extended. I also learned that carrots and tomatoes seemed to have an affinity for each other and so when the tomatoes were set out, there were also a few carrot seeds sown in close proximity.

As the year progressed into spring, there were other "happenings" that made this time of the year by far the most enjoyable for me. Many of these indicators of spring are, sad to relate, missing from life as we experience it today. Who could forget, for example, the hordes of bright yellow butterflies that would make their appearance as the weather gentled? What a beautiful sight they were as they circled the flowers, stopping for a moment to draw their nectar from the blossoms. Then there were frequent visits from the larger brown and bluish-black butterflies, ephemeral creatures whose only mission seemed to be to make the springtime more beautiful. And the honey bees! Someone in the area had a few hives, and it was always a source of delight to watch as the bees collected their pollen. And of course in the afternoon, when the four o'clocks would open, Memere would show us how to take a piece of a particular kind of grass that had a long stem, cut the fuzzy end off, pick the four o'clock blossoms, and string them on the grass stems to make a necklace. As summer approached there would be the fireflies, or, as we called them, "lightning bugs." We would save glass jars, make a few holes in the tin cover, and go out and catch them. When they were caught and put in the jars, they would continue to switch their lights on and off, a never-ending source of delight to us.

But life continues to change. It's been many years since I've seen a swarm of yellow butterflies, and as for the bees, I don't imagine any neighborhood would allow hives to be worked, and I never see any of today's youngsters with a pet June bug. What wonderful pets they made! We would catch the colorful little creatures and attach about a yard of very fine thread to one of the bug's legs. As we walked along, the bug would fly with us, tethered by the thread. When he was tired, he'd return to rest in your hand.

But now let's reminisce about some wonderful cooking, and more specifically about a dish Memere called AUBERGINE TOMATES or eggplant and tomatoes.

| | |
|---|---|
| 3 small eggplants or 2 medium eggplants | 1 16-oz. can Italian tomatoes |
| salt and black pepper | ½ tsp. basil |
| 1 stick butter | ¼ tsp. thyme |
| 2 onions, thinly sliced | 1 tbsp. minced fresh parsley |
| 4 cloves garlic, minced | ¼ tsp. Tabasco |
| | 1 cup grated Swiss cheese |

*Peel the eggplants and then cut them crosswise into slices about 1 inch thick. Season the slices on both sides with the salt and pepper and place them side by side in a large roasting pan. On top of each slice place a small dot of butter. Bake in a preheated 300-degree oven until the slices are soft to the touch, about 1½ hours.*

*While the eggplants are baking, melt ½ stick of the butter in a saucepan over moderate heat and sauté the onions and garlic until the onions are soft. Stir constantly.*

*Simmer the tomatoes in another saucepan for 15 minutes and then add basil, thyme, parsley, and Tabasco. Mix well and remove from the heat; adjust salt and pepper to taste. Now add the sautéed onions and garlic; mix well.*

*Grease a 9" × 13" baking dish; pour half of the sauce into it. Place the baked eggplant slices on top of the sauce, then pour the remaining sauce over the eggplant. On top of this sprinkle the cheese and then dot with the remainder of the butter. Bake in a preheated 350-degree oven for 15 minutes.*

*When ready to serve, place the eggplant under the broiler until the top is brown and crisp. Serves six to eight.*

# CHRIS'S STUFFED EGGPLANT
# WITH CRABMEAT

2 medium eggplants
¼ cup butter
2 stalks celery
6 green onions, finely
chopped
1 onion, finely chopped
4 slices white bread
10 dashes Tabasco
2 eggs, slightly beaten
1 lb. cooked lump or claw
crabmeat (remove any
shells)

salt and black pepper to
taste
¼ cup dry bread crumbs
2 tbsp. grated Parmesan
cheese
½ tsp. paprika
2 tsp. butter

*Split the eggplants in half lengthwise. Place them in boiling water and boil until tender, about 20 minutes. After cooking, remove them from the water and allow them to cool. Scoop out the pulp, being careful not to tear the skin. Chop the cooked eggplant into small pieces and set aside.*

*Moisten the bread with water, then squeeze out excess moisture. Melt the butter in a large skillet. Sauté the celery, green onions, and onion over low heat. Mix in the bread and add the chopped eggplant. Stir and add Tabasco. Remove from the heat and add the beaten eggs, stirring constantly. Now add the crabmeat carefully so as not to break the lumps of crabmeat. Adjust the seasonings; add salt and pepper if necessary. Place the mixture in the eggplant skins. Sprinkle the tops with the bread crumbs, cheese, and paprika. Dot with butter and bake in a preheated 350-degree oven for 20 minutes. Serves six.*

# ED'S MIRLITON STUFFED WITH CRAWFISH

8 mirlitons
1 tbsp. salt
3 qts. water (or enough to cover mirlitons)
1 cup stale French bread
½ cup cold water
4 tbsp. butter or margarine
2 tbsp. oil
1½ cups finely chopped onions
¼ cup finely chopped green onions

1 tsp. sweet basil
pinch powdered thyme
few shakes Tabasco
salt and black pepper to taste
1½ cups boiled and peeled crawfish tails
1 egg, slightly beaten
½ cup bread crumbs

*Place the mirlitons in the salted water. Bring to a boil, and then reduce to a simmer, partially cover the pot, and let simmer for about 1 hour or until tender. Remove from the water and set aside until cool, then cut the mirlitons in half and remove the seed. Remove the pulp with a spoon, leaving about ¼ to ⅓ inch of pulp inside the skin to keep the mirliton halves firm.*

*Soak the bread in water for 5 minutes, then gently squeeze out the water and break the bread into small pieces.*

*Melt 2 tbsp. of the butter or margarine and the oil and sauté the onions and green onions until they are soft. Add the bread and the mirliton pulp to the onion mixture and simmer over moderate heat about 15 minutes. Add the basil, thyme, Tabasco, salt and pepper. Finally, add the crawfish and simmer another 10 minutes. Remove from the heat and stir in the egg until blended. Fill the mirliton shells with the crawfish mixture and sprinkle lightly with the bread crumbs. Dot with the remaining butter and bake in a preheated oven at 350 degrees for 10 minutes. Serves six to eight.*

# SPICY SMOTHERED CREOLE OKRA

"Madder 'n a wet hen" is an expression on which I feel I can expound with a modicum of authority, since Memere always kept a yard full of chickens. It seems that in July or August or some time during the hottest weather, some of the hens would get a notion to set! Now this was past the time, in Memere's opinion, when we wanted any little chickens running around the yard, and so, to discourage any ideas of motherhood, Memere used a procedure that worked nearly every time.

She would fill a bucket with water and bring it into the hen house. Then she would grab the hen setting on the nest and dunk her in the water. When her feathers were thoroughly soaked, the hen would be released in the yard, and boy, was she mad! She would ruffle her feathers, shake herself furiously, and squawk like the dickens! A few treatments like that and the hen would go back to laying eggs, which is what Memere had in mind in the first place.

Now why do I bring up the subject of anger in the chicken yard? Because right now I feel madder 'n a wet hen, and the more I think about it, the madder I get. What I'm concerned about is the manner in which some of our food emporiums are ripping off some of their unsuspecting customers. Case in point: One evening in one of my Creole cooking classes a student approached me with a problem. She had purchased a brisket from one of our best-known supermarkets. She explained that the original weight of the brisket was a little over eleven pounds. After she had trimmed the fat off, the meat weighed exactly six pounds! Imagine buying five pounds of fat at today's prices! A genuine, unadulterated meat scam! What should she do? My advice was to put the meat in a bag and bring it back to the store, confront the manager, explain the problem, and then ask, "What are you going to do about it?" Not "Can you do anything?" or "What can I do?" but a good, strong "What are you going to do about it?"

And while I'm on the subject, I would like to go further. When you buy bagged onions, or potatoes, or carrots, or garlic, or any other prepackaged food, don't for a moment adopt the attitude that you should accept anything but first-class vegetables or fruit. Somehow most of us have developed the feeling that, just because the merchandise has been packaged, and is perhaps a few cents a pound cheaper, we should be willing to accept some of it being not quite up to par. Well, pish, tush, and poppycock (I said I was mad), you paid your money and nothing but class A merchandise is acceptable. As a matter of fact, using good quality raw materials is vital to insure the success of your finished product.

For instance, in this recipe for SPICY SMOTHERED CREOLE OKRA it is important to use only tender, young okra. You can tell this by bending the tips of a few of the okra pods. If the tips snap off, you know the okra is fresh, but if the tips are soft and easily bent and do not pop off, they are not fresh. For the following recipe you may use fresh or frozen okra. It is spicy and a real Creole favorite.

| | |
|---|---|
| **3 lbs. fresh or frozen okra** | **¼ cup water** |
| **6 tbsp. vegetable oil** | **½ tsp. sweet basil** |
| **1 lb. ham, cut in ½ inch dice** | **½ tsp. salt** |
| **1 onion, coarsely chopped** | **¼ tsp. white pepper** |
| **2 lemon slices** | **¼ tsp. cayenne pepper** |
| **1 16-oz. can Italian tomatoes or 3 medium fresh tomatoes, peeled and coarsely chopped** | **2 drops Tabasco** |

*Rinse the okra, cut off the ends, and slice it into ¼-inch pieces.*

*Put 2 tablespoons of the oil in a Dutch oven and sauté the ham and onion until the onion is soft. Remove the ham and onion from the pan and set them aside.*

*Add the remaining 4 tablespoons of oil to the Dutch oven and fry the okra over moderate heat. Add the lemon slices as you fry the okra (the lemon reduces the stringiness of the okra). Sauté 10 or 15 minutes until the okra is no longer sticky and the gummy substance has disappeared. Add the ham, onion, and the tomatoes to the okra. Stir and add the water, basil, salt, white pepper, cayenne pepper, and Tabasco. Cook over moderate heat, stirring frequently, for 15 minutes or until the okra is tender. Remove the lemon slices before serving. Serves eight to ten.*

*NOTE: It is best not to use cast iron for cooking okra, because it will discolor the vegetable.*

# ROASTED, GLAZED, AND STUFFED ONIONS

There were times—when the weather was ideal and the rain was plentiful—that the farmers brought their vegetables to the French Market in such volume that the prices would be considerably reduced. Memere, ever the frugal Creole housewife, always took advantage of the bargains, and we would leave the vegetable stands just loaded to the "gunnels." Now as anyone who has ever read a Creole recipe knows, onions are always an important ingredient in most any dish. So often it was a whole sack of white or yellow onions that we toted home.

Memere would bring along an extra bag, and we'd split the weight, each carrying a bagful of onions. After we got home we went to work on our bargain. The onions were first sorted according to size, rubbed to remove all the loose peeling, and then stored in a dry place. If the weather was cool and the wood stove had been fired up, I knew that part of our newfound onion wealth would wind up as ROASTED ONIONS for dinner that evening. About a dozen medium-sized onions were selected and put in their "jackets" in a baking pan and baked in the oven for about 2 hours. Of course the wood stove had no thermostat, but I would imagine that the onions were baked in a moderate oven (about 325 degrees). When done, they were served just like baked potatoes; you peeled them on your plate and ate them with a little salt and butter.

Of course, when there were plenty of onions in the kitchen, they had to be used before they would spoil, and there were times when Memere would fix her special GLAZED ONIONS. She would do this only when we had brought home white (rather than yellow) onions. She selected a dozen or so of the smallest of the lot. These were peeled, washed, and dried well. Then 2 tablespoons of butter were melted in a skillet, along with 1 tablespoon of oil. The onions were added to the pan and sautéed gently until they were a pale golden color. At this point about 2 tablespoons of sugar was sprinkled over the onions and enough water or stock was added to just barely cover the onions. This mixture was simmered until almost all of the liquid had evaporated and the onions were beginning to be caramelized. They were served immediately.

Ah, but the dish that the whole family really enjoyed most was Memere's STUFFED ONIONS. I'll tell you about it in a moment, but first I've got to give you a remedy for colds that worked every time! Slice 2 large, white onions and place them in a dish. Over the onions sprinkle 2 heaping tablespoons of granulated sugar. Cover and let stand overnight. The next morning there will be a sweet-tasting syrup in the bottom of the bowl, the best remedy for colds ever concocted. Oh, and one more thing, I forgot to mention the price we paid for the onions. Would you believe 2 to 3 cents a pound? Alright, now for the STUFFED ONIONS.

## STUFFED ONIONS

1 doz. medium white onions
4 green onions, finely
   chopped
1 tbsp. minced parsley
6 tbsp. butter
½ lb. chopped ham
½ tsp. salt
½ tsp. black pepper
¼ tsp. cayenne pepper
¼ tsp. white pepper
3 dashes Tabasco
½ tsp. thyme
½ tsp. celery seed
¾ cup seasoned bread
   crumbs

*Peel the onions and place them in a pot of boiling water. Boil until tender (about 10 minutes). With a sharp knife remove enough of the center of each onion to form a cup. Chop the centers you have removed. Sauté the green onions, parsley, and onion centers in the butter. After about 5 minutes of cooking, add the ham and the seasonings, mix thoroughly, and remove from the heat. Add ½ cup of the bread crumbs and mix well. Now fill the onions with this mixture, top with the remaining bread crumbs, and place under the broiler for about 1 minute. Serves four to six.*

# GLAZED ONIONS

**1 doz. small white onions**
**2 tbsp. butter**
**1 tbsp. oil**

**2 tbsp. sugar**
**water or stock**

*Peel, wash, and dry the onions well. Place the butter and oil in skillet and when melted, add the onions and sauté them gently until they are a pale golden color. Sprinkle the sugar over the onions and add enough water or stock to barely cover them. Simmer until almost all of the liquid has evaporated and the onions are beginning to caramelize. Serve immediately. Serves four.*

# ROASTED ONIONS

**1 doz. medium onions (do not peel)**

**salt and pepper to taste**
**butter**

*Place the onions in their "jackets" in a baking pan. Bake for about 2 hours in a 325-degree oven. Serve warm.*

*Each person peels his onions and adds a sprinkle of salt and pepper and a pat of butter. Serves twelve.*

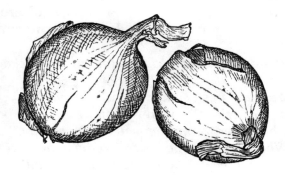

# GLORIA'S POTATOES AU GRATIN

3 tbsp. butter
8 medium Irish potatoes, sliced about ⅛-inch thick
1 tsp. salt
¼ tsp. black pepper

½ lb. grated mild or sharp cheddar cheese
¾ cup whole milk (more, if necessary)

Grease casserole dish with 1 tablespoon butter. Peel and slice the potatoes. Place one-third of the potatoes in the casserole dish. Place one-third of the salt, pepper, remaining butter, and cheese over the layer of potatoes. Repeat the layering process, beginning with potatoes and ending with cheese. Pour milk to just even with the potatoes; if ¾ cup of milk is not enough, add a bit more, but remember you do not want the milk to cover the cheese. Bake in a preheated 350-degree oven for approximately 1½ hours or until the potatoes are tender, the milk has been absorbed, and the top is golden from the melted cheese. Serves six.

# CREAMED SPINACH

2 10-oz. pkgs. frozen spinach or 2 lbs. fresh spinach
4 tbsp. butter
4 tbsp. flour
¼ cup chopped onion

1 cup light cream
⅛ tsp. grated nutmeg
salt and black pepper to taste
¼ cup bread crumbs
¼ cup Parmesan cheese

Cook the frozen spinach as directed on the package and drain well.

If you are using fresh spinach, wash it well.

In a large pot bring 1 gallon of water to a rapid boil. Place the greens in the water. Bring the water back to a boil as quickly as possible. When the water boils again reduce the heat to moderate, and cook uncovered for about 5 minutes or until the spinach is tender. (Test by taste.) Drain the spinach into a colander, rinse gently with cold water, and drain well.

Melt the butter over moderate heat and add the flour to make a roux, stirring constantly, for about 5 minutes. Do not allow the flour to brown. Add the onion and cook until it is soft. Add the cream, nutmeg, and salt and pepper. Reduce the heat to low and simmer for about 3 minutes to remove any uncooked taste from the flour. Now add the spinach and simmer for about 8 to 10 minutes until everything is well mixed. Remove from the heat and cool for about 10 minutes. Pour the mixture into a blender and puree, then spoon it into a buttered casserole dish and sprinkle the top with a mixture of bread crumbs and Parmesan cheese.

This may be made ahead and reheated in a 350-degree oven for 10 minutes before serving. Serves four to six.

## DEBBIE'S SWEET POTATOES

2 cups raw, peeled, grated
   sweet potatoes
½ cup brown sugar
½ cup sugar
3 eggs, lightly beaten
1 cup pecans, chopped
1 tbsp. flour

½ stick butter, melted
dash salt
dash cinnamon
¼ tsp. grated nutmeg
¼ cup bourbon
2 cups milk

Mix all these ingredients. Place in a greased casserole dish. Bake, uncovered, in a preheated, 325-degree oven for 1½ hours or until firm in the center. Serves six to eight.

# HENRI'S PATATES DOUCES FRITES
## (Fried Sweet Potatoes)

4 sweet potatoes
3 tbsp. butter (more, if needed)

sugar (as needed)

*Parboil the sweet potatoes until the tip of a fork can pierce the potatoes, yet they are still firm, then drain. When cooled to room temperature, place the potatoes in the refrigerator for 1 hour.*

*Peel and cut the potatoes lengthwise in ½-inch thick slices. Fry in hot butter until they are brown. Place on a warm platter and sprinkle lightly with sugar. Serves four to six.*

*Note: This is a great accompaniment to Stuffed Pork Chops.*

# SWEET POTATOES À LA LENNIE

4 medium sweet potatoes
3 tbsp. butter or margarine
¼ cup brown sugar
½ tsp. grated orange rind
¼ cup orange juice

½ tsp. salt
8 large marshmallows, halved
½ cup chopped roasted pecans

*Peel, quarter, and boil the sweet potatoes until fork tender. Drain and mash. Blend in the butter or margarine, brown sugar, orange rind, orange juice, and salt. Whip the mixture until it is fluffy, then spread it in a shallow 9" × 13" baking dish. Top with the marshmallows and pecans. Bake in a preheated 350-degree oven for about 20 minutes, until the marshmallows are melted and lightly browned. Serves four.*

breads & grains

Rice is one of the chief ingredients of Creole cooking. Where would our Creole cuisine—our gumbo, etouffée, and jambalaya—be without rice? Rice is versatile; it combines well with vegetables and even leftovers. Try the Creole Rice recipe for a unique blend of tastes and textures.

In this section I have also included such favorites as Banana-Pecan Pancakes and Miracle Bread. You will also find a recipe for making a Pie Crust and one for Hilda's Homemade Noodles. And for a treat your family and friends will not forget, serve Nan's Pizza.

Creoles have always been well known for their breads, batter cakes, and breakfast cakes. It's fun to make your own bread and other baked delights. Besides the wonderful aroma it gives to your home, it satisfies the soul as well as the taste buds. Indulge your family and friends with Chris's Braided Bread, Cinnamon Pinwheels, or Bee's Sticky Buns.

# CREOLE RICE

1 6-oz. box Uncle Ben's Long Grain and Wild Rice
½ cup pine nuts, lightly toasted
1 tbsp. butter plus 3 tbsp. butter
½ cup thinly sliced celery
1 cup sliced fresh mushrooms
⅓ cup partially cooked green beans, cut in 1-inch pieces
¼ cup pickled onions, drained and rinsed in cold water
¼ cup finely chopped green onions, tops only
1 tbsp. minced fresh parsley

*Prepare the rice according to the directions in a large frying pan with a cover. While the rice is cooking, toast the pine nuts in the 1 tablespoon of butter in a heavy skillet, stirring occasionally, over low heat for about 5 minutes or until they are golden. Set aside.*

*Heat the remaining butter in a frying pan; sauté the celery until it is tender yet still crisp; add the mushrooms and the green beans. Stir* gently over low heat until everything is well mixed. When the rice is ready, add the celery-mushroom-green bean mixture to it; then add the pine nuts, pickled onions, green onions, and parsley. Mix everything together gently until it is thoroughly heated. Serves four to six.

# MIRACLE BREAD

2 cups boiling water
2 tbsp. shortening
2 tbsp. sugar
2 tsp. salt
½ cup lukewarm water
2 pkgs. active dry yeast

1 tbsp. sugar
6½ cups flour
1 egg
2 tbsp. milk
sesame or poppy seeds

When the water is boiling, add the shortening, sugar, and salt and then set aside. While this is cooling, add the yeast and sugar to the lukewarm water and then combine with the water-shortening-sugar-salt mixture. Add the flour to this and mix well. Turn the dough every 10 minutes 4 or 5 times to prevent a crust from developing on top of the dough. Divide the dough in half and roll out as you would pie dough; then roll up like a jelly roll. Make diagonal slits across the top of the dough and place on a greased cookie sheet. Let the dough rise about 1 hour or until it is double in bulk. Mix the egg and milk together and brush the tops of the dough with the mixture. Sprinkle with sesame seeds or poppy seeds. Bake in a preheated 425-degree oven for 20 minutes. Yield: 2 loaves.

# HILDA'S HOMEMADE NOODLES

My mother, Hilda Elizabeth Blohm Thompson, was of German descent. Her family served these noodles with such dishes as Chicken Fricassée, Coq au Vin, or pot roast. I lovingly offer my mother's recipe here.

| | |
|---|---|
| **6 eggs** | **¾ tsp. salt** |
| **6 tbsp. light cream** | **4½ cups flour** |
| **¼ tsp. grated nutmeg** | **½ stick butter plus 3 tbsp.** |

*Combine the eggs, cream, nutmeg, and salt and beat thoroughly. Stir in the flour gradually. Work the mixture with your hands until the dough can be rolled in a ball and separates easily from your hands. Knead the dough on a lightly floured surface for about 10 minutes, then divide it into 4 portions. Roll each portion on a lightly floured surface until it is paper thin. Let dry 30 minutes. Use a pasta drying rack if you have one or "make do" with what you have as my mother and my grandmother did. (This was always a comical scene. Picture, if you will, walking into the kitchen and on the back of the chairs, over a large piece of wax paper or a piece of brown paper from a grocery bag, these large ovals of dough hung like laundry drying out. It looked funny, but our taste buds began jumping for joy in anticipation.)*

*When the dough is dry, dust each portion lightly with about 1 tablespoon of sifted flour. Shake gently to remove excess flour. Then roll each piece of the dough like a scroll, and cut with a sharp knife into strips ⅛ to ¼ inches in width. Be careful not to let the dough dry out too much because it will become stiff. Unwind each strip to its full length.*

*Drop the noodles into a large pot of rapidly boiling, salted water. (You will need about 2 quarts of water per portion. Do not crowd the pot.) Stir gently but frequently to keep them separated. A white foam will rise to the surface of the pot; continue to boil for 6 to 8 minutes more or until the noodles are al dente. Drain into a colander. Place the noodles in a bowl and add the butter. Toss gently and serve immediately. Serves eight to ten.*

*To prepare fried noodles:*

*Save ½ cup of the raw noodles to be fried in butter. After unwinding the noodles place them in a large strainer, and shake off excess flour. Fry these in 3 tablespoons butter on moderate heat until they are golden and crispy. Garnish the boiled and buttered noodles with these.*

# NAN'S PIZZA

*To prepare the dough:*

**2 ¼-oz. pkgs. active dry
yeast
1 tsp. sugar
1¼ cups lukewarm water**

**3¼ cups all-purpose flour
1 tsp. salt
¼ cup olive oil**

*Pour the yeast and sugar into ¼ cup lukewarm water (110 to 115 degrees). Let stand for 2 to 3 minutes. Stir the yeast mixture until the yeast and sugar are completely dissolved and set aside in a warm place for 3 to 5 minutes more or until the yeast doubles in volume.*

*Sift the flour into a large mixing bowl and add the salt. Form a well in the center of the bowl and pour in the yeast mixture, 1 cup lukewarm water, and the olive oil. Mix the dough with a fork or with your fingers—I usually start with a fork and work from the center of the well, catching a little flour at a time until I can't use the fork anymore; then I use my fingers to finish mixing. When the dough forms a ball, knead it for about 5 minutes or until it is shiny and slightly sticky. Lightly dust the dough with flour, set it aside in a large clean bowl, and cover with a clean kitchen towel. Let the dough rise 1 to 1½ hours. Makes 2 crusts.*

*After the dough has risen, divide it in half. Place one portion on a 12-inch pizza pan and work it from the center outward until you form a nice crust. Repeat for a second crust or freeze the second half for another time.*

*To prepare the sauce:*

**1 8-oz. can tomato sauce**
**1 6-oz. can tomato paste**
**2 tbsp. sugar**

**1 tsp. of each of these dried herb seasonings: basil, marjoram, thyme, parsley, tarragon, and oregano**
**salt and pepper**

*Pour the tomato sauce, paste, sugar, herb seasonings, and salt and pepper to taste into a medium-size mixing bowl. Mix together well. Preheat the oven to 350 degrees.*

*To prepare the topping:*

**Pepperoni, black olives, mushrooms, onion (or whatever you prefer)**
**¼ cup cheddar cheese**

**¾ cup mozzarella cheese**
**¼ cup grated Parmesan cheese**

*Pour the sauce into the unbaked pizza crust. Use half of the mixture if making 2 pizzas or use it all for a richer single pizza. Top with the cheddar and mozzarella cheese plus the toppings of your choice. (Make it as cheesy as you like! Use 3 parts Mozzarella to 1 part cheddar.) A Soniat favorite is a pepperoni, black olive, mushroom, and onion pizza. Finally, sprinkle generously with the grated Parmesan cheese.*

*Bake at 350 degrees for 20 minutes, then increase the oven temperature to 400 degrees for 10 minutes or until the crust is golden brown and the cheese is bubbling. Remove the pizza from the oven and let it cool for about 5 minutes to let the cheeses set. Then cut and enjoy! Serves four to six.*

*NOTE: To freeze pizza dough, leave it in ball form and place it in a plastic freezer bag. When ready to defrost, remove the dough from the freezer bag, place it in a large, clean mixing bowl, and cover with a kitchen towel. Let the dough defrost and when it is soft enough to handle, knead the dough for about 1 minute. If it is still sticky, add 2 to 3 tablespoons of flour and then place it in your pizza pan. Let it rise for about 1 hour and then proceed with the recipe.*

# PIE CRUST

**1⅓ cups all-purpose flour, plus ½ to 1 cup for flouring board**
**4 tbsp. butter**

**2 tbsp. shortening**
**pinch salt**
**4 tbsp. ice water**
**1 egg, lightly beaten**

*In a large bowl place the flour, butter, shortening, and salt. Using a pastry cutter or two knives, cut in the butter and shortening into the flour and salt until it resembles the size of small peas. Sprinkle one tablespoon water over part of the mixture. Gently toss with a fork, pushing to the side of the bowl. Repeat until all is moistened. Form into a ball. Dust with flour, wrap the dough in wax paper and refrigerate for 30 minutes. Flatten on a lightly floured board and roll dough, from the center to the edges, until dough is ⅛-inch thick and a little larger than your pie pan.*

*Fit the pastry into the pie pan and trim the extra dough hanging over the edge so that it is ¾ inch larger than the pan. Fold the extra dough under along the rim of the pan so that it is double in thickness, then crimp this edge using your thumb and forefinger, press and pinch the dough together spacing evenly around the rim. Prick bottom and sides with a fork for an unfilled crust. Brush with a beaten egg. (If pie shell and filling are baked together do not prick with fork.) Bake at 400 degrees for 10 to 12 minutes or until golden if your recipe calls for baked pastry shell.*

*This crust can be used for a dessert pie or a quiche. Yield: one 9-inch crust or pastry shell. To make two crusts do not double the recipe—follow instructions twice. If you wish to make a 10-inch shell, use 1½ times the preceding proportions.*

# BANANA-PECAN PANCAKES

1½ cups flour
3½ tsp. baking powder
¼ tsp. salt
3 tbsp. sugar
1 egg, well beaten
about 1 cup milk

1 tsp. vanilla
3 tbsp. melted margarine or
  butter
1 large banana, thinly sliced
¼ cup chopped pecans
3 tbsp. vegetable oil

*Sift the flour; measure after sifting. Place in a bowl, and add the baking powder, salt, and sugar. Combine the egg, milk, vanilla, and melted margarine (slightly cooled). The amount of milk you use will depend upon the thickness of pancakes desired; ¾ cup milk will give you thick cakes and 1¼ cups milk will make them quite thin. Pour the liquid mixture into the flour mixture and stir just enough to moisten the dry ingredients. (Do not beat.) Fold in the banana and pecans.*

*Fry on silverstone griddle or a griddle with a non-stick surface for best results. Serve hot with butter and syrup (maple, boysenberry, or raspberry) or honey or hot lemon sauce. (See index for Hot Lemon Sauce.) Yield: about 1 dozen small pancakes. This is a treat you won't forget.*

*NOTE: If you use a griddle with a non-stick surface, you will not need oil.*

# CHRIS'S BRAIDED BREAD

This bread has two purposes: You can eat it yourself or you can give it as a gift at Christmastime. The designs created when the bread is braided are beautiful, and it's definitely delicious to eat.

2 tbsp. dry yeast
¼ cup lukewarm water (not over 100 degrees)
½ cup sugar (honey or maple syrup can be substituted)
¼ cup butter
2 cups milk, scalded and allowed to cool

7 to 9 cups flour (½ bread flour and ½ whole wheat)
3 eggs plus 1 egg
1 tbsp. salt
½ tsp. mace
1 tsp. vanilla
½ cup raisins
½ cup chopped pecans

*Mix the yeast with the lukewarm water and add 1 tablespoon of the sugar. Melt the butter and mix it with the milk and the rest of the sugar. Then stir in the yeast mixture. Add enough flour stirring very well to make a soft, pliable batter. (This batter is known as the sponge.) Set the sponge aside in a warm (not hot) place.*

*Separate 3 eggs and beat the yolks lightly. Beat whites until stiff. Fold the yolks into the sponge first and then fold in the egg whites. Now let the sponge rise until it has doubled in size, about 1 hour.*

*Add the salt, mace, vanilla, raisins, and pecans. After these ingredients are well mixed, start folding in the flour. Keep folding in the flour until the dough is stiff enough to handle. Place it on a floured board and knead well (about 100 to 125 times) until it is smooth and elastic. Place the dough in a greased bowl and cover with a damp cloth. Keep in a warm place, and let it rise again until it has doubled in size. Put the risen dough on the floured board and cut it in half. Cut each half into 7 equal balls of dough. Roll each piece between your hands to form a long rope about ½ to ¾ inch thick and 14 inches long. Place 4 ropes together and pinch the ends together on one end. Braid or plait them and place them on a well-greased cookie sheet. Brush the top lightly with 1 slightly beaten* egg diluted with 2 teaspoons cool water. Then repeat the process with 3 ropes. When you have braided these 3 lengths, place on top of the 4 you have previously braided, pressing the two braids together. Brush the top lightly with the egg and water mixture. Let the bread rise for about ½ hour in a warm place.

Preheat the oven to 300 degrees. Bake for 45 to 50 minutes until well browned. Yield: 2 large loaves.

# CINNAMON PINWHEELS

**3 cups all-purpose flour**
**1½ tbsp. baking powder**
**¾ tsp. salt**
**½ cup margarine plus 3**
  **tbsp. (more if needed)**

**1 cup milk (more if needed)**
**¾ cup brown sugar**
**2¼ tbsp. cinnamon**

Combine the flour, baking powder, and salt. Cut in the ½ cup margarine until the texture is like coarse meal. Add milk until the mixture can be formed into a ball. Turn onto a floured surface, roll the dough out to a ¼-inch thickness. Melt the 3 tablespoons margarine and spread over the dough.

Mix the brown sugar and cinnamon and spread over the dough. Roll the dough tightly and cut into 16 pieces about ½ inch thick. Place the pieces on a cookie sheet or baking pan, leaving space in between each piece because they will spread. Bake approximately 10 to 15 minutes in a preheated 450-degree oven. Yield: 16 pinwheels.

# BEE'S STICKY BUNS

| | |
|---|---|
| 1 cup cake flour | 3 cardamon pods, crushed |
| 3 cups all-purpose flour (more if needed) | ½ cup milk |
| ½ cup sugar | ½ cup water |
| 2 ¼-oz. pkgs. dry yeast | ¼ cup margarine |
| | 2 eggs (room temperature) |

*In a large bowl, mix the cake flour and ⅔ cup all-purpose flour with the sugar, yeast, and cardamon. Combine the milk, water, and margarine in a saucepan and heat over moderate heat until warm (the margarine does not need to melt). Gradually add the liquids to the dry ingredients and beat 2 minutes at the medium speed of your electric mixer. Add the eggs and ½ cup flour, then beat at high speed for 2 minutes. Now mix in enough flour to make a soft dough. Knead until smooth and elastic—about 8 to 10 minutes. Place in a greased bowl and turn the ball of dough over in the bowl so the top of the dough will be greased also. Cover with a damp cloth and let rise in a warm place until the dough has doubled in bulk, about 1 hour. While the dough is rising prepare the topping (recipe follows) and the filling (recipe follows).*

*To prepare the topping:*

| | |
|---|---|
| 1½ sticks margarine | 3 tsp. light corn syrup |
| 1 cup light brown sugar, firmly packed | 1 cup chopped pecans |

*In a saucepan melt the margarine with the sugar and the corn syrup. Beat with a wire whisk until the mixture is thoroughly blended and bubbly. Quickly pour into 3 nine-inch cake pans. (I use foil cake pans, which can be purchased in most supermarkets.) Now sprinkle the chopped pecans in the bottom of the cake pans.*

*To prepare the filling:*

**1 cup brown sugar**
**1½ tbsp. cinnamon**
**½ cup chopped pecans**
**½ cup chopped dates**
   **(optional)**

**1 tsp. grated orange rind**
   **(optional)**
**½ stick margarine**
**¼ cup honey**

*Combine the sugar, cinnamon, and pecans. Include dates and orange rind if you wish. Set aside. Melt the margarine and stir in the honey. Set aside.*

*To assemble the buns:*

*When the dough has risen, punch it down, turn it onto a lightly floured surface, divide it into thirds, cover, and let it stand a few minutes. Roll one piece out into a rectangle 9 by 15 inches. Brush with ⅓ of the margarine-honey mixture, then sprinkle evenly with ⅓ of the brown sugar filling. Roll up to make a cylinder 15 inches long and about 1 to 1½ inches in diameter. Seal the edge by moistening with a little bit of water and pressing the edges together. Cut into 12 pieces and place them in one of the cake pans over the topping. Repeat the process for the remaining two portions of dough. Cover, let rise about 1 hour in a warm place until double in bulk.*

*Bake in a preheated 350-degree oven for 20 minutes. Invert the pans on wire racks. Remove the buns and serve. Yield: 36 buns.*

*Note: If you wish to freeze the buns: Place them (sticky side up) in the pans, cover with foil, and place in the freezer. When frozen remove them from the pans and place them in plastic bags. Keep them in the freezer until you are ready to serve.*

*desserts*

It seems that we all have an irrepressible urge for something sweet—a midmorning or midafternoon snack, or an after-dinner treat to indulge our fancy. The original Creole cooks, being creative and frugal, often combined their interest in sweets with the fruits and nuts that were available to them to produce such favorites as Pecan and Orange Mousse, Pecan Cookies, and Ambrosia. Other kinds of desserts were many and varied. They regularly enjoyed a soft custard dish called Floating Island. The still-popular Creole Custard Pie is the perfect sweet touch to end a luxurious meal.

The Creoles baked fruit pies like Peach Pie or Apple Pie when the fruits were in season. When they couldn't get fresh fruit, they came up with mouth-watering alternatives: Apricot Bars are unusual and very tasty.

Chocolate, the perennial favorite, was also a staple in Creole kitchens, where cooks would create a luscious Chocolate Fudge Cake, a Chocolate Mousse, or a Cocoa Cream Pie. The modern chef may find that Profiteroles au Chocolat are time consuming to prepare, but the reward is well worth the effort.

One of the more unusual fruits in the Creole repertoire is the plantain, a tropical fruit that looks like a large banana. Unlike the banana, the plantain is never eaten raw. To cook, select plantains that are all black and soft to the touch. Fried Plantains were served in my family sometimes as an after-school snack and sometimes as a dessert.

An unusual sweet snack popular with the Creoles years ago was the sweet fried eggplant slices called Aubergine en Farine de Mais. Leon's mother would often cook this for an after-school treat.

In the spring we always looked forward to the appearance of ripe Louisiana strawberries and the many ways we would enjoy them. For an elegant breakfast the sweet luscious berries would be served with softened vanilla ice cream or with Creole cream cheese. (Creole cream cheese is clabbered milk, and it is eaten with rich milk and sugar poured over it. It is only available in the New Orleans area.) As a Sunday treat we would often make fresh Homemade Strawberry Ice Cream in our hand-cranked ice-cream freezer. Everyone took a turn at the crank until the ice cream was frozen. Now we use an electric ice-cream freezer—the task is easier, and the ice cream is just as delicious as always.

With the arrival of hot weather came the ripening of the blackberries. Blackberries were a gift, free for the picking, since they grow wild in any uncleared plot of land. We would go "berrying" and after a short while we had picked enough for a yummy Blackberry Cobbler.

We often make jams and preserves with available fruits. Since we have an abundance of fig trees, there is a bountiful supply of figs in the summer. So we always preserve some to enjoy later in the year as a breakfast treat on toast or crackers or as an evening dessert on cake. I've included a recipe for Fig Preserves from my dear friend Connie Elliott.

New Orleans is known for its celebrations, and the biggest event of all is Mardi Gras and the preceding season. The traditional dessert served throughout the Carnival season is the King Cake. The cake itself is like a coffee cake shaped into a ring and sprinkled with sugar colored purple, gold and green, the official colors of Mardi Gras. Hidden inside each cake is a miniature plastic doll or "baby." The dolls were once made of china or porcelain but are now plastic. Parties are held every week during the season, and the person who is served the portion of the cake with the baby has to host the next party.

Although Creole food is always flavorful, filling, and often quite spicy, we would consider the meal incomplete without a sweet dessert to top it off.

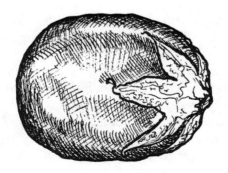

# CHRIS'S PEACH PIE

| | |
|---|---|
| 5 cups sliced fresh peaches | ¼ tsp. ground cinnamon |
| 3 tbsp. pineapple juice | dash salt |
| 1 cup sugar | 1 9-inch lattice-top pie crust |
| 3 tbsp. all-purpose flour | (recipe follows) |
| ⅛ tsp. grated nutmeg | 2 tbsp. butter or margarine |

Slice the peaches and sprinkle them with the pineapple juice. Combine the sugar, flour, nutmeg, cinnamon, and salt; add to the peaches and mix.

Fill the prebaked pie crust with the peach mixture. Dot with butter or margarine. Top with lattice crust. Bake in a preheated 450-degree oven for 10 minutes, then reduce heat to 350 degrees and bake for 30 minutes. Serve warm with whipped cream or ice cream. Serves eight.


To prepare the lattice-top pie crust:

| | |
|---|---|
| 2 cups sifted all-purpose flour | ⅔ cup shortening |
| ½ tsp. salt | 5 to 7 tbsp. cold water |
| | 1 egg, lightly beaten |

Sift the flour and salt together; cut in the shortening with a pastry blender till the pieces are the size of small peas. Add the water, 1 tablespoon at a time, until the dough may be gathered together in one lump.

Divide the dough into 2 portions, one slightly larger than the other. Wrap each ball in wax paper and refrigerate for 30 to 40 minutes.

Roll the larger portion on a floured board, rolling from the center to the edge until the dough is ⅛ inch thick. Place in the bottom of the pie pan and press, fitting the dough in closely so that no air bubbles remain underneath. Trim the pastry ½ to 1 inch beyond the edge of the pan; fold under and flute the edge by pressing the dough with your index finger as you pinch it with the index finger and thumb of the other hand. Brush the crust lightly with the beaten egg.

Bake the bottom shell in a preheated 450-degree oven for 6 minutes.

Roll the second ball of dough onto the floured board and cut into ½-inch strips. Weave the strips of pastry on lightly floured waxed paper and then slip onto the filled baked pastry crust. (To weave the lattice: lay half the strips in one direction, fold alternate strips back as you fit in place the strips that go in the other direction.) After the crust is in place, trim off the ends. Finish the edge by moistening the ends with cold water and pressing down firmly.

## MOTHER'S APPLE PIE

2½ medium apples
1 9-inch pie crust, unbaked
  (see index)
½ cup sugar
½ tsp. cinnamon
¼ tsp. grated nutmeg
1 tbsp. butter
½ tsp. vanilla extract
2 tbsp. water

Peel, core, and quarter the apples. Slice them ⅛-inch thick and in the pie crust arrange them in closely overlapping circles. Also line the apples along the side of the pie crust. Mix together the sugar, cinnamon, and nutmeg and sprinkle this mixture over the apple slices. Dot with butter. Mix together the vanilla and water and spoon evenly over the apple slices. Bake the pie for 35 to 40 minutes at 375 degrees.

This is the perfect "little" dessert when you have only a couple of apples and you want something yummy yet not overly rich. Serves four to six.

# CREOLE CUSTARD PIE

Come back, come back, Mr. Pepitone, wherever you are! Now with a plea like that, you no doubt expect an immediate explanation, and you have my solemn promise that in due time Mr. Pepitone's presence in this recipe will be satisfactorily explained. But first I must tell you what brought all of this on. The other day I had decided that it was time for my monthly shearing, and so I made tracks for the shop of my friendly barber, a craftsman who has been cutting my hair for the past decade. The time was near 10:00 A.M., late enough for anyone to get to work, but my barber shop was closed. One of those little window signs, the kind with the movable hands, told me that my barber would "be back in 15 minutes." Now this is not the first time I have had to cool my heels in the morning sun waiting. So on this day I decided to get my hair cut at some other place. I started on my quest for another barber shop, where I would be able to get just a simple, old-fashioned haircut. But what I was really looking for was someone like my old friend, Mr. Pepitone.

Mr. Pepitone, bless his soul, was the barber who gave me my first haircut. Mr. Pepitone's little shop was located just one block off of Canal Street, in the rear of the building behind Mandina's Restaurant. I was three years old at the time, but I remember the incident as though it were yesterday. At that time, we were living at 232 South Solomon Street and Mr. Pepitone's shop was just a short walk away from home. It was on a Saturday morning that Papete (my father) informed me that I was going to the barber to get my hair cut. I would soon be bereft of (as Mamete, my mother, described them) "my beautiful, blond baby curls." As we walked over to the shop, Papete explained the whole process, and by the time we arrived I had been completely freed of any fear that I might have had. As we entered the shop Mr. Pepitone took me by the hand and showed me around. He let me inspect the scissors and clippers and combs and the shelves filled with shaving mugs, each mug for a specific customer. And then we sat down for the haircut. I say *we* because Papete sat down first and I sat on his lap. It was a day I have never forgotten, even to the stick of licorice that I received when the job was done. As time passed and until we moved from our Solomon

Street address, my monthly haircut money went to my friend, Mr. Pepitone. Even years later, when I was in the neighborhood and needed a haircut, I would visit the old shop just to listen to Mr. Pepitone talk while he snipped and clipped. So here's to old-time barbers, may their tribe increase!

Thinking about the "good old days" reminds me of something else I loved in my childhood, CREOLE CUSTARD PIE.

*To prepare the pie crust:*

| | |
|---|---|
| **½ cup sugar** | **1 tsp. baking powder** |
| **⅓ cup shortening** | **¾ tsp. nutmeg** |
| **1 egg** | **pinch salt** |
| **1½ cups flour** | |

*Mix the sugar and shortening together until creamy. Beat the egg until frothy and add the egg, flour, baking powder, nutmeg, and salt to the sugar mixture. When well mixed, knead slightly for a minute (don't overwork) and then with your rolling pin, roll out the dough a little bit larger than the size of your pie plate. This crust will be fairly thick (about ¼ inch). Gently place the crust in the pie plate. Prick the bottom of the pastry shell with a fork and bake in a preheated 400-degree oven for 8 to 10 minutes or until light brown.*

*To prepare the filling:*

| | |
|---|---|
| **1 cup milk** | **½ cup sugar** |
| **2 eggs, beaten** | **⅛ tsp. salt** |
| **3 tbsp. flour** | **1 tsp. vanilla extract** |

*Mix ⅓ cup of milk with the beaten eggs, flour, sugar, and salt. Bring ⅔ cup of milk to a boil in a saucepan over moderate heat. Now slowly stir the egg mixture into the boiling milk and lower the heat to a simmer, stirring constantly. Simmer slowly until thick, then remove from the heat and stir in the vanilla. Pour the mixture into the crust and bake in a preheated 400-degree oven until the top is golden brown, about 35 minutes. Serves six.*

# PROFITEROLES AU CHOCOLAT

½ cup butter
1 cup boiling water
1 cup all-purpose flour

¼ tsp. salt
4 eggs

*Add the butter to the boiling water in a heavy-bottomed saucepan; boil slowly until the butter is melted. Reduce the heat to low; add the flour all at one time and the salt and stir vigorously, over low heat, until the mixture forms a ball and leaves the sides of the pan.*

*Remove the saucepan from the heat; cool slightly. Now make a hole in the center of your paste and add the eggs, one at a time, beating after each addition for a few seconds until the egg has been absorbed.*

*After the last egg has been added beat until the paste is smooth and glossy. Drop by tablespoonful 3 inches apart on a greased cookie sheet. Bake in a preheated 425-degree oven about 25 to 30 minutes or until they are golden brown, puffy, and doubled in size. They should be firm and crusty to the touch. Pierce the side of each puff with a sharp knife and set the puffs back in the warm oven (with heat turned off) for 30 minutes, with the oven door halfway open. Remove them and cut in half horizontally; set aside until thoroughly cooled. Fill with Bavarian Cream Filling (recipe follows).*

*To prepare the Bavarian Cream Filling:*

3 tbsp. unflavored gelatin
6 tbsp. cold water
2 cups milk
¾ cup sugar
¼ tsp. salt

6 eggs, separated
¼ cup confectioners' sugar
2 cups heavy cream
1 tsp. vanilla extract

Soften gelatin in the cold water. Scald milk in the top of a double boiler. Add the gelatin, sugar, and salt; stir until dissolved. Beat the egg yolks slightly; stir in a little of the hot milk mixture. Now stir the egg-milk combination into the remaining hot milk mixture. Cook over hot, not boiling water until slightly thickened (4 to 5 minutes), stirring constantly. Remove from the hot water and cool.

Beat the egg whites, gradually adding the confectioners' sugar until it forms soft peaks. Fold the stiffly beaten egg whites into the custard, folding it in gently; continue folding in gently until custard is well mixed. Set the custard in the refrigerator to cool.

Whip the cream until it is doubled in volume and forms soft peaks. Fold the whipped cream and the vanilla into the chilled custard. Spoon the Bavarian Cream into the thoroughly cooled cream puffs. Refrigerate until ready to serve.

To prepare the chocolate sauce:

**1½ cups sugar**
**3 tbsp. cornstarch**
**3 oz. unsweetened chocolate**

**3 cups boiling water**
**6 tbsp. butter**
**1½ tsp. vanilla extract**

Combine the sugar, cornstarch, and chocolate in a heavy saucepan. Add the boiling water and simmer for 1 minute, stirring constantly; then add the butter. Stir well until the butter melts, then add the vanilla. Set aside, but keep warm.

When you are ready to serve the profiteroles, spoon the warm sauce over the cream puffs. Yield: 2 dozen.

# NECTARINE CREAM CHEESE PIE

1½ cups peeled, thinly
   sliced nectarines
2 tbsp. pineapple juice
1 9-inch pie crust, unbaked
¾ cup sugar
¼ tsp. grated nutmeg

pinch salt
6 oz. cream cheese
2 eggs, beaten
½ cup cream
1 tsp. vanilla extract

*Slice the nectarines and place them in the pineapple juice for 15 minutes, until you are ready to begin assembling the pie.*

*Drain the nectarines, discard the liquid, and arrange the slices in the pie crust. Mix ¼ cup of the sugar with the nutmeg and sprinkle over the nectarines. Bake in a preheated 450-degree oven for 15 minutes. Remove from the oven and turn the heat down to 350 degrees. Cream together the remaining ½ cup sugar, the salt, and the cream cheese. (If the cheese is allowed to soften in advance, it will cream more easily.) Add the eggs and mix until smooth. Add the cream and vanilla, mix well, and pour over the nectarines in the pie shell.*

*Bake in the 350-degree oven for 40 minutes. Serves six to eight.*

# SHIRLEY'S COCOA CREAM PIE

½ cup cocoa
1¼ cups sugar
¼ tsp. salt
⅓ cup cornstarch
1 tsp. gelatin

3 cups milk
3 tbsp. butter
1½ tsp. vanilla
1 9-inch pie crust, baked

Combine the cocoa, sugar, salt, cornstarch, and gelatin in a medium-sized saucepan. Slowly blend in the milk, stirring until smooth. Cook over moderate heat, stirring constantly, until the filling boils; boil 1 minute. Remove from the heat; blend in the butter and vanilla, and pour into the pie crust. Chill 3 or 4 hours.

You can garnish with dollops of whipped cream and top with a cherry. Serves six to eight.

# CHOCOLATE FUDGE CAKE

Every year, shortly after Twelfth Night, the excitement would start to build; the days leading up to Mardi Gras were filled with a frenzied anticipation. First we had to decide what our costumes would be. Have you ever heard of a yama-yama suit? That was what we would wear most of the time. A yama-yama suit, as we knew it, was a clown suit, and I guess since it was the easiest thing to construct, we usually wound up being clowns. Memere would be the one to cut out and sew up the costumes, but first there was the trip to the store for the necessary "goods." It was a short walk to Rougelot's, our favorite department store, and there the process of selection began. If my memory is correct, the material out of which most of the costumes were made was cambric. This seemed to be ideal, since the cloth was thin, easy to work with, and had a delightful sheen. The customary clown collar ruffs were stiffened with a piece of buckram (I'm digging deep to remember those names). The colors we chose ranged from combinations of purple and gold to black and orange. After a few days of cutting and sewing and fitting, our costumes were complete. Papete, who had a sort of artistic flair, was called on to design the clown hats, which usually turned out to be cardboard cones. After the cones were made and fitted to our heads, Memere would cover them with cloth, add a few streamers, and the hats were finished. Then there were a few little decorative touches like small bells sewed to the puffed-up imitation buttons, ruffs around the ankles and wrists, and we were almost ready. Oh, another important thing about our yama-yama suits—they were always made a few sizes too large just in case we had to wear a lot of extra clothes on Mardi Gras day. (It has been known to be freezing!) But we still needed masks (in those days everyone wore a mask), and so back to the store we went.

And so the great day finally arrived. My sister Blanche and I rose early in anticipation of the big day. We were already decked out in our yama-yama suits and waiting for the rest of the family.

Many things had to be done. Memere was preparing the potato salad, a large bowl of which would accompany us as we set out for the Mardi Gras parades. Soon the baskets were packed with food and a marvelous assortment of goodies, and off we went to the Mardi

Gras! Where we lived was just a short walk over to Claiborne and Elysian Fields, where we would get our first glimpse of what were probably the most magnificent costumes of the entire Carnival. Yes, I'm referring to the Indians. The trek of the Indians would usually start just about at Elysian Fields Avenue on to Claiborne to Canal and, of course, they would walk the entire distance to allow the onlookers to admire the marvelous work that went into their outfits. So as we stood waiting for the Claiborne streetcar, we would catch sight of the Indians, singly or in groups, as they made their way to the Mardi Gras. Once in the streetcar it was a short ride to our destination, to St. Philip Street just off Claiborne. There lived Mamete's three "old aunts," Taté, Adele, and Nanan, and that's where we would settle for part of the day, where we would deposit the food and other paraphernalia. After a short walk we would be on Canal Street and in the very thickest part of the revelry.

It seems that in those days there were a lot more maskers. (Of course there were, there were no truck parades and so the costumed revelers would walk the streets.) On Canal Street it was one magnificent mélange of color with wall-to-wall people from Claiborne to St. Charles. By 9:30 in the morning the whole family would establish itself as close as possible to the parade route, and then it was a process of standing and waiting for the pièce de résistance, which, of course, was the Rex parade, followed by that indescribable spectacle called Zulu. Ah, but soon the parades would end (I point out that there were only four parades per season—Momus, Proteus, Rex, and Comus—a meager pittance compared to what we enjoy today) and when the parades were over, we would retreat to our base on St. Philip Street to eat and rest for a time before returning to the same location that evening to witness the Comus parade. Then it was back home to bed, and the next morning to church for the ashes on the forehead that ushered in the Lenten season. Now at the beginning I mentioned the goodies we carried to the Mardi Gras. One of our favorites was Mamete's CHOCOLATE FUDGE CAKE.

Here's a cake that, believe it or not, makes its own frosting as it bakes!

⅓ cup shortening
1 cup sugar
3 tbsp. light cream
1 tsp. vanilla
2 1-oz. squares unsweetened chocolate, melted and cooled
1 egg

1¼ cups sifted all-purpose flour
½ tsp. baking soda
1 pinch salt
¾ cup water
½ cup semisweet chocolate pieces
½ cup chopped walnuts

*Mix the shortening, sugar, and cream in a bowl until light and fluffy. Mix in the vanilla and cooled chocolate. Now add the egg, beating well. In another bowl sift together the flour, baking soda, and salt and add to the creamed mixture alternately with the water, beating after each addition. Spread the mixture in a greased, lightly floured 9" × 9" × 2" baking pan. Sprinkle the chocolate pieces and the chopped walnuts over the top. Bake in a preheated 350-degree oven until done, about 30 minutes. Allow to cool in the pan before serving. Serves six to eight.*

# KING CAKE

New Orleans is known for its celebrations; the biggest celebration of all is the period before Mardi Gras—our Carnival season. One important food tradition throughout the Carnival season is King Cake. The festivities begin on January 6, Twelfth Night, a feast day of the Roman Catholic church. This day commemorates the visit of the three wise men of the east to the baby Jesus. The King Cake honors the three kings; each cake has a doll or "baby" hidden inside. Traditionally the person who receives the portion of cake with the baby is designated host for the next party. Parties are held each week between Twelfth Night and Mardi Gras. The cake itself is like a coffee-cake shaped into a ring and decorated with sprinkles of sugar colored purple, gold and green, the traditional colors of Mardi Gras.

2 ¼-oz. pkgs. dry yeast
¼ cup lukewarm water
1 tsp. sugar plus 6 tbsp.
1 cup milk, scalded
2 eggs, beaten, plus 1 egg yolk
1½ cups sifted flour plus 2 to 2½ cups
3 tbsp. melted butter plus 2 tbsp.

1 tsp. vanilla extract
1 tsp. orange extract
1 tsp. salt
⅛ tsp. grated nutmeg
1 tbsp. water
⅓ cup light corn syrup
2 drops each purple, green, and gold food coloring

*Dissolve the yeast in the water and add the teaspoon of sugar.*
*Scald the milk and let cool, then add the ½ cup of sugar, the eggs and 1½ cups of the sifted flour. This is what is called a "sponge." This is the first process in baking bread. Cover with a damp cloth and let the sponge rise in a warm place until it doubles in size. This will take from ½ hour to 1 hour.*
*When the sponge is ready, add the 3 tablespoons of melted butter, vanilla and orange extracts, salt, and nutmeg. Mix well. Add the 2 cups of the sifted flour and mix thoroughly until the dough comes away from the sides of the bowl and does not any longer stick to your hands. Knead about 10 minutes or until smooth and shiny.*

*Place dough in a warm greased bowl and brush the surface very lightly with melted butter; cover with a damp cloth and let rise in a warm place (80 to 85 degrees) about 2 hours or until doubled in bulk.*

*Turn out on a floured board and roll the dough with your hands into a rope one inch in diameter. Transfer to a well-greased cookie sheet and form the rope of dough into one large or two small oval-shaped cakes. Join ends by moistening with water.*

*If you want to put a bean or doll in the cake, press it into the dough at this time. Cover and let rise ½ hour. Brush with egg yolk diluted with 1 tablespoon of water.*

*Bake in a preheated 325-degree oven for 20 minutes.*

*Add 2 drops of one of the food colorings to 2 tablespoons of sugar, and stir quickly until the sugar is evenly colored. Proceed with the two remaining colors and set aside.*

*Remove from the oven and decorate by brushing the top of the cake with corn syrup and alternating 3-inch bands of purple-, gold-, and green-colored granulated sugar—the traditional colors of Mardi Gras. When the cake cools, you're ready for the party! Serves eight to ten.*

## AUNT KATE'S PECAN COOKIES

**4 cups chopped pecans**
**2 cups sifted powdered**
  **sugar**
**½ cup flour**

**2 tsp. baking powder**
**1 tsp. vanilla**
**4 egg whites, stiffly beaten**

*Mix the pecans with the sugar; add the flour and baking powder. Continue to mix well as you add the vanilla, then fold in the egg whites. Drop by the half-teaspoonful on a greased cookie sheet. Bake about 1 hour in a 250-degree oven until light tan in color. Yield: 2 dozen.*

# APRICOT BARS

It was just about the middle of May when the little yellow blossoms were appearing on our tomato plants and white blossoms on the peppers, while slender chive shoots were thrusting upward in anticipation of being chopped and sprinkled over a delicious, cold vichyssoise. It was also "good weather time," a time when plans were made for a weekend trip to Spanish Fort and "over the Rhine." The preparations were started the evening before. Fishing lines, crab nets, plates, forks, knives, and spoons were packed and ready. Come early Saturday morning and all the food had to be prepared. Memere and Mamete, in the kitchen, would be putting together a picnic feast that would last the whole day. Pepere had a great liking for omelet sandwiches and so they were made and wrapped. The omelets had a scattering of sautéed green onions in their middle; placed between buttered halves of French bread, they were practically irresistible. Then there were the cheese sandwiches: flavorful Swiss on rye and crumbly Limburger spread on a black bread Memere would get from the French Market, with thinly sliced onions spread over the cheese. Papete's particular favorite was Roquefort cheese, and so a wedge and some soda crackers always found their way into the basket. For meat there were always a number of kidney chops that were panfried to a delicious brown and carefully cradled between buttered slices of French bread. Oh, the smells of that kitchen!

But soon everything was packed and we were ready to go. The liquid refreshment? That certainly was not neglected. There was homemade root beer in large jars with cracked ice; also, a jar of lemonade and, of course, for the adults, a mite stronger libation. A piece of waterproof oilcloth would be used to chill a bottle of wine and a few bottles of home brew. Some of the ice from the refrigerator was chopped and put into the oilcloth. This was wrapped around the wine and beer and carefully laid in the bottom of the baskets, and then we were off to the Fort! Down to Claiborne and Elysian Fields we would march, the whole family, to board the Claiborne streetcar. The fare was seven cents and so the whole family rode for less than fifty cents. At Canal Street we made a transfer and got into the Spanish Fort car. As I remember it, the car pulled a trailer and we would always try to get into the trailer. It was more fun, we thought. In a short time we were at the picnic grounds, at the site of the Old Spanish Fort, Bayou St. John and the Lakefront. Blankets and tablecloths were spread under the trees and the fun would start. There were games and eating, fishing and eating, crabbing and eating, and, of course, our trip "over the Rhine." Now, I'm digging back into some rather hazy memories, but I seem to remember a wooden bridge over the Bayou; on the other side was a sort of carnival with rides, games, and places where food and drink could be found. I remember, years later, one of the old structures still standing was known as Tujague's. It was a place that featured food, drink, and music for dancing. But back we went to the other side again to fish or crab a little more and eat a little more; then, for dessert, Memere would proudly uncover a pan of her APRICOT BARS.

| | |
|---|---|
| 1 cup dried apricots | 1 cup light brown sugar |
| 1 stick butter, softened | 1 tsp. baking powder |
| 4 tbsp. powdered sugar | 1 pinch salt |
| 1⅓ cups sifted flour | 2 tsp. vanilla extract |
| 2 eggs, beaten | ½ cup chopped walnuts |

Cover the apricots with water and bring to a boil. Boil for 10 minutes, then drain and chop. Place the butter in a bowl and mix well with the sugar and 1 cup of the flour. Pour this mixture into a greased 8" X 8" pan, pat down, and bake for 25 minutes in a preheated 350-degree oven.

Add the brown sugar to the eggs and stir until sugar is thoroughly dissolved. Mix the remaining ⅓ cup flour with the baking powder and salt; add to the brown sugar and eggs. Mix in the vanilla extract, walnuts, and chopped apricots, and then spread over the baked layer in the pan. Return to the oven and bake for another 30 minutes. Allow to cool in the pan and then cut into squares. Yield: 12 bars.

# FRIED PLANTAINS

2 plantains (black and soft
to the touch, but not
mushy)
3 tbsp. butter

sugar
2 tbsp. water
1 tbsp. rum (optional)

*Peel the plantains, splitting them lengthwise; cut them in thirds. Sauté them in butter over moderate heat until they are golden and a fork easily pierces them. Remove them to a warm platter and immediately sprinkle generously with granulated sugar.*

*Deglaze the pan with a tablespoon or two of water and, if you desire, one tablespoon of rum. Reduce the syrup by half and pour it over the plantains. Serves four to six.*

# AUBERGINE EN FARINE DE MAIS
## (Eggplant in Cornmeal)

This is a very old, quick Creole dessert.

1 small eggplant, peeled
and thinly sliced
1 cup yellow cornmeal

pinch salt
3 tbsp. vegetable oil
¼ cup sugar

*Peel the eggplant and slice lengthwise. Soak 30 minutes in cold, slightly salted water. Add a pinch of salt to the cornmeal. Drain the eggplant and dip the slices in the cornmeal.*

*In a heavy skillet fry the eggplant in the oil until they turn golden brown and crisp. (Do not crowd the frying pan.) Immediately sprinkle the slices with sugar. Serves six.*

# FESTIVE AMBROSIA

In the fall, the delicious Louisiana citrus crops of navel, satsuma, and mandarin oranges are harvested. This harvest coincides with the availability of newly fallen pecans; we combine these items with coconut and any other fresh fruit we can find—such as apples, cherries, and grapefruit—to make our version of AMBROSIA, "the nectar of the gods."

1 large, ripe pineapple or 1 20-oz. can pineapple chunks
6 sweet Louisiana or navel oranges
½ cup powdered sugar
1 tsp. grated orange rind
1½ cups coarsely chopped pecans

1 small coconut, grated
¾ oz. Cointreau
¾ oz. orange curaçao
2 cups whipped cream
Maraschino cherries (garnish)

*If you are using fresh pineapple, peel and cut it into bite-size pieces. Peel the oranges, being careful to remove all the white membrane. Then slice the oranges ¼ inch thick and remove the seeds. Mix the orange rind with the chopped pecans.*

*Place in a large glass bowl one layer of oranges, sprinkle with the sugar, some of the chopped pecans, then a layer of pineapple and then a layer of coconut. Repeat until all are used. Pour over this mixture the Cointreau and curaçao. Marinate at least 2 hours or overnight in the refrigerator before serving.*

*When you are ready to serve, spoon fruit into individual glass bowls. Top the fruit with a dollop of the whipped cream and then add a maraschino cherry in the middle of the whipped cream and sprinkle with chopped pecans. Serve immediately. Serves eight to ten.*

# BLACKBERRY COBBLER

*To prepare the biscuit topping:*

**1 cup all-purpose flour**
**2 tbsp. sugar**
**1½ tsp. baking powder**
**¼ tsp. salt**

**¼ cup butter**
**¼ cup milk**
**1 egg, lightly beaten**

*Sift together the flour, sugar, baking powder, and salt. Cut in the butter until the mixture resembles coarse crumbs. Combine the milk and egg, then add them to the dry mixture; stir just enough to moisten.*

*To prepare the filling:*

**4 cups fresh blackberries**
**½ cup water**
**2 tbsp. sugar**

**1 tbsp. cornstarch**
**1 tsp. vanilla**

*Soak the berries in cold salted water for 15 to 20 minutes. (This is necessary to rid the berries of any tiny worms.) Scoop the berries out of the water and rinse them again (be careful not to crush them) and then drain.*

*In a saucepan combine the water, berries, sugar, cornstarch, and vanilla; bring to a boil, then reduce to simmer, stirring constantly until the sauce has thickened.*

*To assemble the cobbler:*

*Pour the filling into 1¾-inch high baking dish 8¼ inches in diameter. Immediately spoon on the biscuit topping in 6 mounds. Bake in a preheated 400-degree oven for 20 to 25 minutes. Serve warm with cream or ice cream. Serves six.*

# FLOATING ISLAND

3 eggs
2 tbsp. sugar plus ½ cup
1 qt. milk
1 vanilla bean or ½
  teaspoon vanilla

¼ tsp. salt
1 tbsp. cornstarch
½ cup shredded coconut

*Separate eggs. Beat egg whites until stiff; slowly add the 2 tablespoons of sugar, and beat vigorously. Heat the milk and the vanilla bean, if you are using one. Bring to a simmer. Now drop the egg whites by spoonfuls into the hot milk allowing 3 minutes on each side and turning once. Remove the egg whites from the milk with a skimmer and set them aside.*

*Mix the ½ cup of sugar, salt, and cornstarch, and add to lightly beaten egg yolks. If you are using a vanilla bean, remove it at this time. Pour the hot milk over the egg yolk mixture, then cook over low heat in a double boiler. Stir and cook until the mixture thickens. Remove from the heat, and add the coconut and vanilla extract if needed. Spoon into individual bowls and gently spoon the meringue islands over the top. Serve cold with Raspberry or Amaretto Sauce (recipe follows). Serves four to six.*

# AMARETTO OR RASPBERRY SAUCE

½ cup sugar
¼ cup water

2 tbsp. amaretto or
  raspberry liqueur

*In a small heavy saucepan combine the sugar and water. Bring to a boil over moderate heat, stirring to dissolve the sugar. Boil for 1 minute. Remove from the heat, and let cool for at least 10 minutes. Stir in the liqueur. When serving the FLOATING ISLANDS ladle on sauce as desired.*

# PRUNE WHIP ELEGANTE

Memere always said that for a dish to taste good it had to look good. Mamete agreed and whatever they cooked flattered the palate but also appealed to the eye. This skill and artistry was developed through many, many years of practice in the kitchen for both of them. Memere, I might add, had been at a certain point in her life a professional cook, and this experience carried over in her home meal preparation. Mamete had been orphaned in her preteen years, and her experience was cooking as a small girl for a large family accustomed to the haute cuisine of the Creoles. From such experiences it was inevitable that each would develop into an accomplished cook.

I remember Mamete, for example, being able to place a tomato in the palm of her hand and, with a very sharp knife, slice the fruit horizontally right down to a single, thin slice in her hand. She would do the same with an onion when she made an onion salad or soup. I have not yet been able to develop that confidence!

But I began by propounding the idea that food should look good to be enjoyed, and so I refer back to the slicing of the tomatoes and onions to point out that the slices were very thin and uniform, a pleasant sight to behold. I also remember when Memere made her noodles. After she had rolled her dough to a paper thinness, she would fold the dough and cut her noodles with a sharp knife. You could bank on it that there wasn't a hair's difference in the width of the noodles. This looked so much more enticing than sitting down to a plate of noodles of varied widths and thicknesses.

And how about those apple pies? Well, one thing that enhanced their appeal was the latticed cover. The strips were thin and uniform, a sheer delight to eat. When a piece of meat was cooked, it was properly trimmed and any gristle or nerve running through the meat was removed. And I remember those "heavenly hashes" Memere would make with her leftover soup meat and potatoes. All the meat that went into the frying pan was cut to the same length, and the potatoes were cubed with not the slightest variation in the size of the cubes. A small thing, you might say, but this was indicative of the painstaking effort put forth by cooks who were proud of everything they turned out. I remember that whenever Mamete or Memere made an aspic, at the bottom of the mold there would always be a decoration made of slices of lemon or egg and strips of green onion or carrots. When the aspic was unmolded, the decoration was on top. As for ordinary everyday cooking, it was always garnished with minced parsley or parsley sprigs, or maybe the bright red of a few strips of pimento. I can see Memere now, with a small paring knife, taking a few scrapes of butter and winding up with a butter rose. But the way she served her poached red snapper was a work of art! After the fish was poached, it would rest on lettuce leaves in the platter. The skin was peeled off, and then Memere would carefully remove every bone in the fish. (I have tried many times to do this, but so far, no success.) Now while the fish rested in its boneless splendor, Memere would very thinly slice a half dozen radishes. A little mayonnaise would be brushed over the fish and then the fish scales would be reconstructed with the little radish rounds. From the tail right on up to the head the radish slices were placed, overlapping just like the original scales, and the effect was absolutely magnificent!

Speaking of works of art, here's a recipe that elevates the prosaic prune into an elegant dessert.

| | |
|---|---|
| **1 cup prunes** | **3 egg whites** |
| **3 thin slices lemon** | **¼ tsp. salt** |
| **1⅓ cups water** | **¼ cup chopped pecans** |
| **¼ cup sugar plus 2 tbsp.** | **6 to 8 tbsp. whipped cream** |
| **1 tbsp. lemon juice** | **2 tsp. currant jelly** |

*Simmer the prunes and the lemon slices in the water for 45 minutes to 1 hour or until very soft. For the last 5 minutes add the ¼ cup of sugar, reduce heat to low and stir occasionally. Drain and mash thoroughly through a sieve.*

*Combine the prunes and the lemon juice; beat until very well blended. Chill for one hour.*

*Beat the egg whites with salt until soft peaks form. Gradually add the two tablespoons of sugar and continue to beat until stiff peaks* form and the surface is smooth. Fold the prune mixture into the egg whites. Add the chopped pecans and spoon into six to eight parfait or sherbet glasses. Chill.

Serve with a dollop of whipped cream and on top of the cream add ¼ teaspoon of jelly. Serve with ladyfingers. Serves six to eight.

Sit back, and relax as you and your guests enjoy this simple but elegant dessert.

This was a favorite of my very dear friend—Betty Hoffman. It saddens me to state that death came to her before my book. This one is for you, dear Betty, and for Fran and Buddy Hoffman.

# CHOCOLATE MOUSSE

**12 oz. semisweet chocolate**
**2½ tsp. unflavored gelatin**
**3 tbsp. water or amaretto**
**3 eggs plus 2 egg whites**

**1½ cups whipping cream**
**3 tsp. vanilla**
**3 tbsp. sugar**

Melt the chocolate in a double boiler and stir. Measure the gelatin and mix it with the liquid (water or amaretto); stir until gelatin is softened and set aside.

Separate the eggs and beat the 3 egg yolks until they are light and frothy. Add the whipping cream and blend. Cook the yolk mixture over low heat, stirring and watching carefully just until the mixture coats the back of a spoon. Remove from the heat, cool slightly, and stir in the softened gelatin. Add the vanilla and the melted chocolate.

Beat the 5 egg whites until they begin to form soft peaks. Add the sugar very slowly as you continue to beat the whites. Fold the egg whites into the chocolate mixture and spoon into a serving dish. Refrigerate. Serves six.

# PECAN AND ORANGE MOUSSE

1 cup sugar
3 tbsp. grated orange rind
½ cup boiling water
1 ¼-oz. pkg. unflavored
  gelatin
¼ cup cold water

1 cup orange juice
¼ cup lemon juice
¼ tsp. vanilla extract
1 cup whipping cream,
  whipped
1 cup chopped pecans

Combine the sugar, grated orange rind, and hot water; boil for 1 minute. Soften the gelatin in the cold water for 5 minutes, then dissolve it in the hot syrup. Add the orange and lemon juices. Chill in refrigerator until slightly thickened, then beat the gelatin mixture until it is light and fluffy. Add the vanilla, then fold in three-fourths of the whipped cream and ¾ cup of pecans. Spoon into parfait glasses or trifle bowl. Refrigerate for 2 hours. Garnish with the remaining whipped cream and pecans. Serves four to six.

# HOMEMADE STRAWBERRY ICE CREAM

It was a very pleasant conversation I had the other day. I had just met a gentleman, who, right after we were introduced, informed me that he was a fan of mine and an admirer of Creole cuisine. That's always nice to hear, and so I inquired about his interest in cooking. He informed me that he was a transplanted northerner who thought New Orleans cooking was the best in the world. Then he went on to tell me how intrigued he had been with the area from the first day he arrived in New Orleans.

"Here was a state, the only one in the United States, that didn't have counties but parishes.

"Parish," he said, "seemed to be so much nicer a word than county."

I went on to explain that our parishes were originally ecclesiastical divisions and that this was the way the state had been divided. Then he made another observation I found very interesting. "Where I came from we divided the year very differently from the way you New Orleanians do," he said. "We were always cognizant of the vernal equinox, the summer solstice, and, of course, the autumnal equinox and the winter solstice. But here these divisions mean nothing."

I thought about that for a moment and then I had to agree that he was absolutely right. What always ushers in our spring is not an equinox, but the arrival of the first sacks of crawfish! You can bet that when the pecan trees begin to show their leaves and the mud bugs begin to arrive in the market—or to go after our baited nets in droves—we don't need any groundhog to prognosticate on the arrival of spring. Then of course there is another season: Carnival. Everybody knows about and participates in this one!

I started to think back on past seasons. It was just after the crawfish season was in full bloom that the early fresh vegetables were beginning to make themselves seen in the market and the good vegetable dishes made their way to the table. During the Lenten season and on to the beginning of summer the prices of the fruits and vegetables would come way down. Soon the watermelon season was on. Vacation was coming soon and the crabs and fish were starting to bite at the lake, and soon it was out to Milneburg. There was also the strawberry season when we waited for the berries to arrive from Hammond and Ponchatoula. The summertime treat was a freezer full of strawberry ice cream. But as the summer waned, no thought was ever given to the autumnal equinox; instead we concentrated on the vines on which the mirlitons were ripening. This was also the season for trips to the lake with the cast net for bringing in a few pounds of fresh shrimp. And as the chill in the weather began there was the sausage season and a good time for hogshead cheese, and, of course, the beginning of the duck season. And so the year went and the only thing we had to wait for was Papa Noël and then the beginning of the new crawfish season. Simple, wasn't it? Well, maybe not quite so uncomplicated, but as I bade my new friend good-bye, I left with a warm glow inside as I went over in my mind how Memere used to express it when she would observe how *"le bon Dieu* must have loved the Creoles so much to give them everything they needed and in such abundance right here in La Belle Nouvelle Orleans."

As I said, we always waited eagerly for the strawberry season to get those luscious berries from Hammond and Ponchatoula so that we could make HOMEMADE STRAWBERRY ICE CREAM.

| | |
|---|---|
| **6 eggs, separated** | **1 qt. fresh strawberries** |
| **2 cups sugar** | **2 tbsp. lemon juice** |
| **1 qt. whole milk** | **1 cup whipping cream** |

*Put lightly beaten egg yolks, 1 cup of the sugar, and the milk in a heavy-bottomed saucepan, and mix well. Bring to a simmer over moderate heat, stirring constantly. Simmer for approximately 15 minutes until the liquid coats the back of a spoon, then remove from the heat and cool.*

*Wash the strawberries in another bowl, mix in the remaining cup of sugar, and stir in the lemon juice. Add this mixture into the milk and egg mixture and stir well; add the whipping cream.*

*Beat the egg whites until they form stiff peaks and then add them to the cream and strawberries. Now pour the mixture into a one-gallon electric ice cream freezer. The cylinder holding the cream mixture should be filled only three-fourths full. Serves eight to twelve.*

# CONNIE'S FIG PRESERVES

**5 lbs. figs**                    **1 lemon, sliced**
**5 lbs. sugar**

*Select ripe but firm figs with stems. Wash them individually, then place them in a large bowl and cover with sugar. Set the bowl on a countertop overnight; syrup will form. The next day place the figs and syrup in a large heavy-bottomed pot. Add the lemon slices, and cook over very low heat until the syrup thickens (about 1 hour) and the figs are soft and dark amber in color. Pack hot in sterile Mason jars, making sure the rims of the jars are free of syrup or fig seeds.*

*Yield: about 5 pints.*

*Note: There may be a difference in the amount of syrup the figs make so you may end up with more syrup than is needed to fill the jars. Extra syrup is delicious served over pancakes or waffles.*

# HOT WINE PUNCH

Every year, about a week before Christmas, when everything around the house seems to be wrapped in ribbons and bright paper, we set up the Christmas tree and I'm always given the task of hanging the fifteen thousand (or so it seems) lights that will illuminate its branches. It's about this time when words like "Bah, humbug!" and "It's all a big commercial promotion" begin to creep into the tunnels of my mind.

I remember how, one year, Willie the Robot would stare at me as I walked through the living room; made me feel darned uncomfortable! And I recall the awful time I had trying to remove Glop Glop, the Amorphous Monster, from the living-room rug! It's then that I begin to conceive the fiendish idea of buying only toys that will self-destruct the day after Christmas. And my incipient Noelaphobia begins to break out when I begin to total up in my mind the cost of the gifts I have bought and I realize that I will need to strike oil in the backyard in order to live free and clear of debt in the upcoming year.

But as all this flashes through my mind, something wonderful seems to compete with these thoughts. It's the remembrances of Christmases past. It's the remembrance of awakening early on Christmas morning and jumping up and running to see what had been left the night before. The empty stockings that had hung from the mantel were now filled with nuts and candies and fruit. And then I began a search for the skates that I'd written Santa for and the cap pistol, and it was a frantic clawing at wrapping paper and pulling string and ribbons to get to the goodies within the packages. Remember those wonderful feelings, dear friend? I remember how my mother and father would just beam every time I squealed with delight as I opened another package. As I seem to remember, just about every toy was already assembled so there was no interminable wait for Papete or Pepere to find their toolbox to put together my Christmas presents. These are the feelings that seem to take over whenever I begin to pull for the Grinch to be successful in his attempts to spirit Christmas away. And of course, as I ran through the kitchen, Memere and Mamete were basting the turkey and chopping the vegetables for the soup and draining the oysters for the patties and the pies were cooling, having been taken from the oven earlier. Well, I sincerely hope that you have had similar experiences and that when you're just about ready to blast that little old man off your chimney, you revert to empathizing with yourself in your own remembrances of Christmases past. As Memere used to say, "Papa Noël will be here soon."

On Christmas evening, when everyone was exhausted from Yule activities, Memere would expend just a little more of her inexhaustible supply of energy and come up with a HOT WINE PUNCH, which, being a special occasion, the children were allowed to sample.

¾ cup powdered sugar
½ cup water
1 lemon, thinly sliced
1 orange, thinly sliced
10 whole cloves
1 cinnamon stick (about 2 inches)

juice of 1 grapefruit (about a cup)
juice of 2 large oranges (about a cup)
1 pt. burgundy or claret

*Put the sugar, water, lemon, orange, cloves, and cinnamon stick in a saucepan. Bring to a boil and let simmer for 5 minutes. Now add the grapefruit and orange juices. Bring back to a simmer and add the wine. Reheat and then strain through a cheesecloth and serve; a fitting climax to your Joyeux Noel. Serves six.*

# MERLE'S FESTIVE PUNCH

This is my friend Merle Guerin's punch recipe. We use it at all our festive celebrations. Once you have tried it I'm sure you'll adopt it, too.

2 46-oz. cans pineapple juice
1½ cups lemon juice
1 cup lime juice
1 12-oz. can frozen orange juice concentrate
2 cups sugar

2 1-liter or 33.8-oz. bottles ginger ale
2 1-liter or 33.8-oz. bottles carbonated water
2 fifths pink champagne
1 fruit ice ring (recipe follows)

*Combine the juices and sugar and chill. Just before serving add the ginger ale, carbonated water, and champagne. Pour over ice or a fruit ring. Serves fifty.*

# FRUIT ICE RING

2 6-oz. pkgs. pink lemonade mix
1 20-oz. can pineapple slices

1 20-oz. can peach slices
6-oz. jar red cherries

*Make the lemonade.*
*Fill 2 3½-cup ring molds with a small amount of the lemonade. Add one layer of the pineapple slices, then place a cherry in the center of each slice. Freeze until firm, then add a layer of peach slices. Cover with a little more lemonade and freeze this layer until firm. Repeat until fruit and lemonade fill the mold.*
*When you are ready to serve the punch unmold the fruit ice ring and place the ring in the center of the punch bowl. It will keep your punch cold and as it thaws will enhance the flavor of the punch*

*rather than diluting it.  Add the second ring when the first one has melted.*

  *The fruit ring takes a day or two to prepare so make it ahead of time.*

# index